Literacy Activity Book

Year 4

Ray Barker and Louis Fidge

EDUCATIONAL

Every effort has been made to trace copyright holders and to obtain their permission for the use of copyright material. The authors and publishers would gladly receive information enabling them to rectify any error or omission in subsequent editions.

Acknowledgements
The authors and publisher are grateful for permission to reproduce the following text:

the extract from *Catchpole* by David Oakden, published by Methuen Children's Books (a division of Reed International Books Ltd); the extract from *Fanny and the Monsters* by Penelope Lively, published by William Heinemann (a division of Reed International Books Ltd); the extract from *The Working Children* by Wes Magee, ©Wes Magee; the extract from *Ninny's Boat* by Clive King (1980) reproduced by permission of David Higham Associates Ltd; the extract from *The Greek News*, text ©1996 Anton Powell and Philip Steele, reproduced by permission of the publisher, Walker Books Ltd., London; *Peter's Pets* © David Orme, first published in *Poetry Express*; the extract from *The Lion, The Witch and the Wardrobe* by C.S. Lewis, by permission of HarperCollins Publishers Ltd; the extract from *Blue Misty Monsters* by Catherine Sefton, published by Faber and Faber, by permission of David Higham Associates Ltd; *Sugarcane* by John Agard, published by The Bodley Head in *I Din Do Nuttin'*; the extract from *Tom's Midnight Garden* by Phillipa Pearce, by permission of Oxford University Press; *My Future* by David Harmer, from *Earthways, Earthwise*, selected by Judith Nicholls, by permission of Oxford University Press; the extract from *Technology in Ancient Egypt* by Judith Crosher and the extracts from *Spotlights – The Egyptians* by Neil Grant, published by Macdonald Young Books, an imprint of Wayland Publishers Ltd; the extract from *Leila* by Sue Alexander and George Lemoine, first published in the United States as *Nadia the wilful* by Pantheon Books, by Patheon Books, reprinted by permission of Curtis Brown Ltd; the extract from *Hurt* by Janina Amos, published by Cherrytree Press Ltd; *All Fools' Day* by John Agard in *I Din Do Nuttin'*, published by The Bodley Head, by permission of Random House; the extract from *Isimeme Stories* by Isimeme Ibazebo published by Spindlewood; the extract from *John and the Green Dragon* from *The Orange Tree and Other Stories* by Jamila Gavin published by Methuen Childrens Books, by permission of David Higham Associates Ltd; *Geraldine Giraffe* by Colin West.

First published 1998
10 9 8 7 6 5 4 3 2

Letts Educational,
The Chiswick Centre, 414 Chiswick High Road, London, W4 5TF
Tel: 020 8996 3333
Fax: 020 8742 8390

Text © Ray Barker and Louis Fidge
Designed, edited and produced by Gecko Limited, Bicester, Oxon

Illustrations © Kiran Ahmad, Sally Artz, Jonathan Bentley (Beint & Beint), Liz Catchpole, John Eastwood (Maggie Mundy Illustration), David Frankland (Artist Partners), Shelagh McNicholas, Robert McPhillips, Chris Molan, Dave Mostyn, Jan Nesbit, Martin Sanders, Jamie Sneddon, Andrew Warrington.

British Library Cataloguing-in-Publication Data
A CIP record for this book is available from the British Library
ISBN 1 84085 064 7
Printed in Italy by Rotolito Lombarda

Letts Educational is part of the Granada Learning Group. Granada Learning is a division of Granada plc.
Visit www.letts-education.com for free education and revision advice.

Introduction

The Literacy Textbooks:

- support the teaching of the Literacy Hour
- help meet the majority of the objectives of the National Literacy Strategy Framework
- are divided into 3 sections, each sufficient for one term's work
- contain ten units per term, each equivalent to a week's work
- provide two Self Assessment units in each term to check on progress

- contain two Writing Focus units each term to support compositional writing
- include a Glossary of definitions of terms used in the book
- list High Frequency Words at the back of the Year 3, 4 and 5 textbooks
- provide coverage of a wide range of writing, both fiction and non-fiction, as identified in the National Literacy Strategy Framework.

Unit number →

Text for reading and discussion

Key teaching points

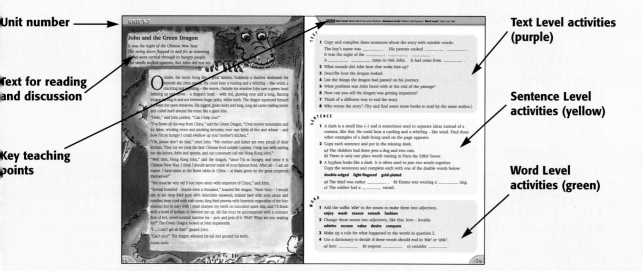

Text Level activities (purple)

Sentence Level activities (yellow)

Word Level activities (green)

Self Assessment units:

- appear after every five units
- review the key objectives at Sentence Level and Word Level in the preceding five units
- contain a spelling chart to support the teaching of spelling strategies
- may be used to provide:
  - a review of progress when completed and kept as a record
  - further practice in areas of concern
  - homework assignments.

The Glossary:

- explains and gives examples of key words and concepts
- may be used for teaching purposes or for reference by the pupil.

Writing Focus units:

- appear after every five units of work
- develop work covered in the preceding five teaching units
- support work on compositional writing
- contain support for the teaching of different essential writing skills, e.g. how to plan a story.

High Frequency Word lists:

- contain words that occur frequently in children's reading and writing
- help children to recognise these words and to spell them correctly
- are often referred to and used in the activities in the book
- provide an easily accessible resource for spelling activities.

	Text Level	**Sentence Level**	**Word Level**
	Focus		

	Text Level	**Sentence Level**	**Word Level**
Term 1	• Characterisation, historical settings	Verbs	Synonyms, common letter strings
	• Characterisation, setting, playscripts	Punctuation, editing and revising	Common phonemes
	• Characterisation, historical settings	Verb tenses	Spelling rules (verbs – past tense)
	• Playscripts	Verb tenses (past, present and future)	Syllables
	• Characterisation, historical settings	Commas	Suffixes

Writing Focus 1.1   Storyboards; Story patterns; Playscripts; Turning stories into plays; Handy hints for playscripts

Self Assessment 1.1   Review of Word and Sentence Level skills Units 1.1 – 1.5; Handy hints on spelling

	• Text organisation, purpose, audience	Subject/verb agreement	Dictionary skills
	• Non-fiction text	Paragraphs, main ideas	Definitions, homophones
	• Poems with a similar theme	Adverbs	Past tense of irregular verbs
	• Text organisation	Comparison of narrative/information texts	Proofreading
	• Features of instructional texts	Adverbs	Suffixes (adverbs)

Writing Focus 1.2   Writing an interview; Writing a magazine article; Writing reports; Handy hints on editing your work

Self Assessment 1.2   Review of Word and Sentence Level skills Units 1.6 – 1.10; Handy hints on spelling

Term 2	• Expressive and descriptive language	Types of adjectives, phrases	Common word endings
	• Setting, characterisation, similes	Nouns and adjectives, synonyms	Spelling strategies
	• Characterisation, settings and themes	Word order in sentences	Common word endings
	• Poetry from a different culture	Comparing adjectives	Syllables, suffixes
	• Poetry from different times	Comparative adjectives	Suffixes

Writing Focus 2.1   Descriptive language; Planning stories; Writing for an audience; Handy hints on reviewing your work

Self Assessment 2.1   Review of Word and Sentence Level skills Units 2.1 – 2.5; Handy hints on spelling

	• Character and setting	Apostrophes	Old-fashioned vocabulary, gender
	• Use of language, structure	Adverbs, apostrophes	Over-used words, prefixes/suffixes
	• Features of explanatory texts	Commas, connectives	Proofreading
	• Explanatory texts	Word order	Spelling strategies
	• Contents page, Index, Glossary	Apostrophes (possession), punctuation	Root words

Writing Focus 2.2   Note-making; Using diagrams; Explaining clearly; Writing poetry; Handy hints on writing a poem

Self Assessment 2.2   Review of Word and Sentence Level skills Units 2.6 – 2.10; Handy hints on spelling

Term 3	• Cultural setting, paragraphing	Classes of words, suffixes	Compound words
	• Cultural setting, relationships, issues	Suffixing	Diminutives
	• Social issues, relationships	Making nouns/adjectives	'wa', 'qua', 'wor'
	• Cultural setting, poetic terminology	Types of sentences	Investigating 'k' and 'v'
	• Cultural setting, paragraphing	Punctuation, verbs and prepositions	'ss' and 'll'

Writing Focus 3.1   Reviews; Developing stories; Stories with a moral dilemma; Handy hints for planning stories

Self Assessment 3.1   Review of Word and Sentence Level skills Units 3.1 – 3.5; Handy hints on spelling

	• Points of view, presentation	Structuring arguments	'tion', 'sion', 'ssion'
	• Moral dilemmas and solutions	Dashes and hyphens	'able' and 'ible'
	• Evaluating advertisements	Colons/semi-colons	Common letter strings
	• Poetic terms and features	Conjunctions	Root words, spelling strategies
	• Persuasive writing	Positive and negative statements	Spelling strategies

Writing Focus 3.2   Points of view; Advertisements; Types of poetry; Handy hints on drafting and editing

Self Assessment 3.2   Review of Word and Sentence Level skills Units 3.6 – 3.10; Handy hints on spelling

CONTENTS

Strange Happenings at Night

Outside the gate it was dark, then as the noise inside gradually died away, it became very quiet. A nightingale began to sing but flew off as Catchpole, heart thumping madly, skidded across the drawbridge. There was a soft plop as a water rat slid from the bank into the moat, leaving ripples spreading in the moonlight. Catchpole clawed his way up an elm tree and lay panting on a thick branch. It was time to think.

An hour passed. Catchpole was still thinking as all around him the night forest came alive. There were squeaks, flutterings and barks. The grass below the tree rustled with passing mice and hedgehogs. A mole came up with a worm in its mouth, looked round and dived back into the rich earth. Somewhere an owl hooted mournfully.

Gradually Catchpole became aware that other things, strange things, were happening in the forest as well. From not far away he could hear the murmur of men's voices and an occasional clink like a sword tapping against armour. He climbed higher up the tree and from the topmost branches he suddenly saw a light appear on the castle battlements. It shone faintly, disappeared and then shone again. After a few seconds the same thing happened – light, dark, light. Catchpole's heart leaped. Someone inside was signalling to someone outside.

It took several minutes for Catchpole to reach the place where he had heard voices. He peered out from under a bush and saw a group of men, dressed in dark clothing, all armed with swords or spears. One of them, taller than the rest and with a great red beard, was speaking in a low voice.

"Two flashes," he said. "That means that she knows we're here. Now watch. Count the flashes again."

From Catchpole *by David Oakden*

T

1 At what time of day did the story take place? How do you know?

2 *a)* Who is the main character? *b)* Who, or what, do you think Catchpole is?
   How can you tell?

3 Where does the story take place (its setting)?

4 As the story begins, do you think Catchpole is inside or outside the castle?
   Say why.

5 Where was Catchpole? How was he able to see what was going on?

6 How long was Catchpole in the tree before he heard voices?

7 *a)* How are the men dressed? *b)* What are they carrying?

8 Who do you think they are signalling to? Why?

9 What do you think will happen next? What will Catchpole do?

10 Name the parts of the castle that are mentioned in the text. Explain what you
    think they are. (Check in a reference book on castles if you can.)

NTENCE

1 Copy and complete these sentences with suitable verbs.
   a) Catchpole <u>crossed</u> the drawbridge.   *b)* Catchpole _____ a tree.
   c) An owl _____ .   *d)* Catchpole _____ some voices.

2 Think of suitable verbs for the way these animals move, e.g. Mice <u>scamper</u>.
   a) Birds _____ .   *b)* Horses _____ .   *c)* Worms _____ .

3 Copy and complete this definition: A verb is ...

R D

1 Look in Set B and find the 'partner' for each word in Set A with the same letter
   string. Write the pairs of words like this: catch – snatch.

Set A	catch	strange	mice	came	could	mail
Set B	twice	failure	snatch	change	blame	would

2 Add one more word to each pair of words containing the same letter string.

3 Think of as many synonyms as possible for each of the verbs below,
   e.g. run: race, scamper, speed.   **say   get   find   like   think   see**

4 Use the *Look, say, cover, write, check* method to help you learn the words.

7

Excuses, Excuses

Time: Present day

Place: Dad and Amy are talking to each other in the kitchen.

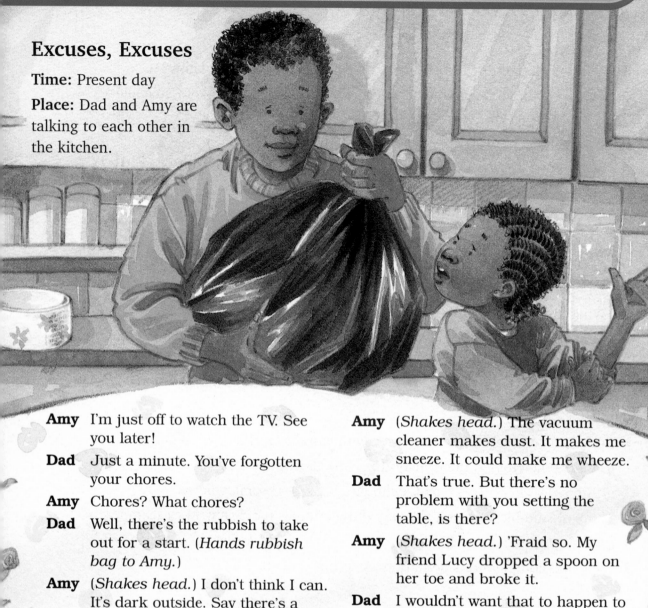

Amy   I'm just off to watch the TV. See you later!

Dad   Just a minute. You've forgotten your chores.

Amy   Chores? What chores?

Dad   Well, there's the rubbish to take out for a start. (*Hands rubbish bag to Amy.*)

Amy   (*Shakes head.*) I don't think I can. It's dark outside. Say there's a ghost?

Dad   Don't be so silly. Well, tidy up your computer games instead.

Amy   (*Shakes head again.*) I saw a big spider in the box where I keep my computer games, I think it must be the biggest spider in the world.

Dad   Oh, I forgot. You can't stand spiders? Well, vacuum the carpet in the lounge then. (*Opens cupboard door and points to vacuum cleaner.*)

Amy   (*Shakes head.*) The vacuum cleaner makes dust. It makes me sneeze. It could make me wheeze.

Dad   That's true. But there's no problem with you setting the table, is there?

Amy   (*Shakes head.*) 'Fraid so. My friend Lucy dropped a spoon on her toe and broke it.

Dad   I wouldn't want that to happen to you.

Amy   We could make some chocolate chip cakes.

Dad   Oh no, I don't think so. I'll be too busy doing all your chores. There's no time to make cakes.

Amy   Guess what? My fear of the dark and spiders and dropping spoons has disappeared! And I can hold my nose so I don't sneeze when I'm using the vacuum cleaner.

Dad   Good idea. Let's get on with the chores, then we can make some cakes. (*They smile at each other.*)

1 Who are the two main characters in the play?

2 What is the setting for the play (where does it take place)?

3 Which of these adjectives would you use to describe Amy's Dad?

bossy   patient   angry   understanding   short-tempered

4 Describe what sort of a girl you think Amy is.

5 In what way was Dad clever at solving the situation?

6 *a)* What is an excuse? *b)* Do you think Amy really was scared of all the things she said? Why? *c)* Do you think her dad really believed her excuses? Why?

7 *a)* How can you tell it is a play? *b)* How do the actors know what to do?

8 If someone who lived 100 years ago was able to read this play, there would be some things they would not understand. Make a list of them.

1 Rewrite the play as dialogue. Punctuate it correctly. Try not to use the verb 'said' too often. Set it out like this:

"I'm just off to watch the TV. See you later!" Amy called.

Dad replied, "Just a minute. You've forgotten your chores."

2 When you have finished the dialogue, underline each verb in it.

3 Check what you have written to: *a)* make sure it makes sense *b)* correct any spelling or punctuation mistakes *c)* change anything you are not happy with.

1 Match up the pairs of words that rhyme, e.g. stood – could.

Set A	stood	chore	side	ghost	shake	clean
Set B	saw	ache	could	been	coast	tried

2 Underline the common phoneme in each pair of words, e.g. d<u>ir</u>t – h<u>ur</u>t.

3 Add one more rhyming word to each pair.

4 Use the *Look, say, cover, write, check* method to help you learn the words.

5 Make up six sentences and use some of the words from Set B in them.

Fanny has Lunch with Papa

They went home. Papa was in a most genial mood and allowed them to stop for a few minutes to throw stones in the village pond, and made no comment when Albert climbed upon the stone wall beside the lane and walked along it. Fanny wished that she could follow him but knew what was allowed – at a pinch – to boys was certainly not allowed to a girl wearing her best Sunday dress and coat. She wished, also, and that too not for the first time, that she was a boy.

At home, the Young Children were just being unloaded from the donkey cart, at the end of their outing. Fanny hugged the donkey and the donkey, who never showed his feelings, except for a general impression of gloom and suffering, stood in resignation, while she buried her face in the thick dusty fur of its neck.

The Young Children were taken up to the nursery while Fanny, Albert and Emma went with Papa into the dining room for Sunday dinner. One of the only things in favour of being an Older Child, Fanny considered, was that you were allowed into the dining room for Sunday dinner with the grown-ups. Not only did this make you feel interesting and important (even if you did have to pay more than usual attention to good manners), but the food was better. There was no tapioca or semolina, but things like roast beef and Yorkshire pudding. Fanny licked her lips in happy anticipation as she sat down in her place, lowered her head while Papa said Grace, and raised it again as he picked up the carving knife to sharpen it. There was the most exquisite smell of roast lamb, and, as the green baize door to the kitchen swung to and fro behind Mary the parlour maid, gusts of something else delicious that she could not for the moment recognise.

They ate. Papa asked them questions about what they had learned in the schoolroom with Miss Purser this week. He was still in a very good humour and only once told Albert to sit up straight and not speak with his mouth full. Fanny, agreeably stuffed with roast lamb, forgot most of her troubles, such as Miss Purser's sums and the passage from the Bible that she would certainly not be able to recite this evening, and chatted to Papa about one thing and another. The roast lamb was taken away to the kitchen and Papa asked Mary to bring in the next course.

From Fanny and the Monsters *by Penelope Lively*

T

1 What clues are there that tell you:
   a) Fanny came from a large family;
   b) the family was rich; *c)* Fanny's father
   was a stern parent; *d)* the story did not
   take place in the present time; *e)* boys
   were treated differently to girls?

2 In what ways is Fanny's life different
   from yours? In what ways is it similar?

3 Why do you think the Young Children
   were taken to the nursery and not
   allowed to eat with the others?

4 What can you learn about transport
   at this time?

5 The children's mother is not
   mentioned in the passage. Suggest a
   reason why this might be.

6 Write some sentences showing the
   order in which things happened in the
   passage. Do it like this: The children
   stopped to throw stones in the village
   pond for a few minutes. Albert
   walked on a wall.

TENCE

The passage below has been written as if the story is taking place in the present.

On the way home Albert <u>climbs</u> on the wall and <u>walks</u> along it. The young
children <u>travel</u> home in the donkey cart. Fanny <u>gives</u> the donkey a hug. The older
children <u>go</u> into the dining room. Fanny <u>sits</u> down at her place. She <u>licks</u> her lips.
Papa <u>says</u> Grace. He <u>picks</u> up the carving knife and <u>sharpens</u> it. The maid <u>comes</u>
in from the kitchen with the meat.

1 Write the passage again. Change the verb tenses from the present tense to the past
   tense like this: On the way home Albert <u>climbed</u> on the wall and <u>walked</u> along it.

2 Now write it in the future tense, like this: On the way home Albert <u>will climb</u> on
   the wall and <u>will walk</u> along it.

D

1 Write the past tense of these regular verbs by adding the suffix 'ed'.
   Do it like this: I walk – I walked. Make up a rule for what you discover.
   I look   I show   I load   I lick   I ask   I wish

2 Write the past tense of these regular verbs by adding the suffix 'ed'.
   Do it like this: I try – I tried. Make up a rule for what you discover.
   I cry   I carry   I bury   I hurry   I worry   I empty

3 Write the past tense of these regular verbs by adding the suffix 'ed'.
   Do it like this: I hug – I hugged. Make up a rule for what you discover.
   I tap   I chat   I hum   I stop   I beg   I slap

The Working Children

Time: A century ago (Victorian times)

Place: A busy street.

People pass along the street. Harry and Beth, two hungry urchins, try to attract their attention.

Harry	Spare a farthing! Give us a farthing!
Beth	Anything for a starving girl? A crust of bread?
1st lady	(*pointing*) Just look at those children! Just look at their clothes!
2nd lady	Call those *clothes*? Nothing but rags, filthy rags.
1st lady	And their feet are bare. And what *horrible* feet! Ugh!
2nd lady	Don't go near them. You'll catch a disease. Come on.

(*They pass by. A grim-looking man stops and then walks slowly round the children, as if inspecting them.*)

Scragscutt	And who are you two, eh? What's with this shouting, eh?
Harry	We're begging, sir. We're hungry. This is my young sister, Beth, and she's –
Beth	Starving!
Scragscutt	Hungry, are you? Starving, eh? And what are your parents doing about it? Why aren't they looking after you, eh?
Harry	Our parents are dead, sir. We're orphans.
Scragscutt	Orphans, eh? And you've got no money.
Beth	That's right, sir.
Scragscutt	Well, maybe I can help you. Have you … er … ever worked?
Harry	Worked? No, sir. We're too young.

Scragscutt	Oh, you're never too young, lad. Maybe I can teach you to work. Yes, I'm sure you'd like to earn some money … and to have a good dinner, wouldn't you, eh?
Harry	Oh, yes, sir.
Scragscutt	And how old are you?
Harry	I'm nine –
Beth	And I'm eight.
Scragscutt	Just right! Just the ticket! Look, you two youngsters follow me and I'll … er … find a place for you to stay. And I'll … er … find you a job of work. Heh, heh! You'll soon learn how to work, how to work hard! You call me Scragscutt. That's all you need to know. Just follow me.

Wes Magee

1 *a)* When does the play take place? *b)* Where does the play take place?
c) Where did you find the answers to (a) and (b)?

2 Write all the facts you can discover about Harry and Beth from the introduction, from what the children said and from what others said.

3 How does the writer of the play make you feel about *a)* Harry and Beth *b)* the two ladies? Give your reasons.

4 What are the main differences between Fanny (in Unit 1.3) and Beth?

5 *a)* What can you learn about Scragscutt from the play?
b) Why do you think he took such an interest in the children?

6 Write a few sentences and explain how you think the story continues.

TENCE

1 Copy the sentences below. Underline the verb in each sentence. (Note that sometimes a verb is one word, e.g. We <u>looked</u>. Sometimes there are two words, e.g. We <u>are looking</u>.) Say if the verb is in the present tense or past tense.

Do it like this: We <u>are looking</u>. Present tense

a) We are begging.   *b)* I ran fast.   *c)* They were sitting.   *d)* He looks dirty.
e) Are you an orphan?   *f)* She was cold.   *g)* The girl stood up.   *h)* It is raining.

2 Rewrite each sentence. If a verb is written in the present tense, change it into the past tense. If a verb is written in the past tense, change it into the present tense.

3 Write these sentences in the future tense:
a) I ran fast.   *b)* He looks dirty.   *c)* She was cold.   *d)* The girl stood up.
e) They notice Beth.   *f)* Harry shivered.

RD

1 Say these words. Listen to how they can be broken into two parts (syllables). Copy each word and then write it in syllables. Do it like this: became = be + came.

hungry   urchin   farthing   children   filthy   disease   slowly   shouting

2 Find three words in the play that can be broken into three syllables.

3 Look at the words in Term 1 of the High Frequency Word List, page 96. Find and write ten words with *a)* two syllables *b)* three syllables.

4 Two-syllable words with a double consonant in the middle, may be split into syllables like this: bub – ble. Split these words into syllables in the same way:

kettle   common   fiddle   buffer   dagger   pillow   hammer   winner   popping

Ninny is Taken Prisoner

I showed him the gold chain around my neck. That was another mistake. He almost pulled my ears off as he stripped it from me.

"Take him as your slave, Wulf," the Myrging leader said to a young man. The young man tore the two gold brooches out of my robe. I had to tie it in a knot to keep it up. It was so grubby with mud from the pond and moss from the tree that it wasn't worth stealing.

"Those Angle-folk won't come back for this," said the man called Wulf, looking down his nose at me. Of course they were talking in their own language now, but it wasn't all that different and I could understand what they were saying.

"Offa will come back," I said. "He doesn't waste words."

Wulf gave me a clip round the ear, and his heavy shield to carry. We trailed over the heath towards the forest.

The gloomy forest trees closed over our heads. At least the everlasting wind seemed to stop, down here, but I could hear it sighing in the treetops. Little hard things came rattling down from the trees above. I stopped to pick some up, and hid them in the pocket of my smock, but Wulf shouted at me to come on.

Firelight twinkled through the tree-trunks. We came to a clearing, with rough huts in it. Wulf led me to one of them. A bony woman came out. She looked at me.

"What's that you've got?" she asked Wulf.

He said, "A thing to wash the dishes."

"You might have got me a bigger one," she sniffed.

I breathed the good meaty smells coming from cooking pots over the fires. The woman made me fetch more firewood. The Myrgings ate, but no food came my way.

"Clean that out," the woman said, pointing to a cooking pot. It was what I had been waiting for. At least I'd get some scrapings. But I'd hardly got a mouthful or two on the end of a piece of bark before they dragged me to the fire and put me in front of their leader.

From Ninny's Boat *by Clive King*

T

1 *a)* Who was captured?   *b)* Who captured him?   *c)* Where did it happen?

2 *a)* What was the name of Ninny's people? *b)* Who was their leader?

3 How can you tell that Ninny was quite wealthy?

4 *a)* Who became Ninny's master?   *b)* How did he treat Ninny?

5 *a)* Explain what a slave is. (Use a dictionary to help if necessary.)
   b) What job was Ninny given? *c)* Why do you think Ninny was called 'a thing'?
   d) How do you think Ninny felt about becoming a slave?

6 Write some things you have discovered about the way people lived at this time.
   Write about: *a)* their clothes *b)* weapons *c)* jewellery *d)* homes *e)* how they cooked.

7 Think how the story might continue. Write the conversation Ninny might have
   had with the Myrging leader.

NTENCE

1 Copy and punctuate these sentences from the passage, using commas correctly.
   a) offa will come back I said   *b)* we came to a clearing with rough huts in it
   c) clean that out the woman said pointing to a cooking pot
   d) take him as your slave wulf the myrging leader said

2 Copy these sentences and put in the missing commas.
   a) Out of the forest came a huge hairy angry bear.
   b) Mr Smith who was an old man had to sit down slowly.
   c) If you turn right you will soon reach the house.
   d) George bold and brave captured the dangerous lion.

RD

1 Make these verbs into nouns by adding the suffix 'ment', like this: punish – punishment.
   advertise   commence   encourage   manage   move

2 Use a dictionary. Write a definition for each noun you have made.

3 Write these adjectives in four sets according to their suffixes:
   **accidental   watery   foolish   dirty   angelic   childish   musical   athletic
   metallic   boyish   furry   national   angry   natural   volcanic   girlish**

4 Now write the words above again. Write the root word from which each adjective
   is made. Do it like this: accidental – accident.

5 Complete these words by adding the suffix 'hood', 'ship' or 'ness':
   man _ _ _ _   friend _ _ _ _   good _ _ _ _   wicked _ _ _ _   child _ _ _ _

15

Storyboards

Storyboards are a good way of helping you plan a story.

Scragscutt meets Beth and Harry begging.

He takes them to his house.

He makes them work as chimney sweeps.

They manage to escape, and …

1 Use the storyboards to help you write a story. Make up a happy ending for it!

2 Divide a page into four. Draw four storyboards to retell the passage in Unit 1.3. Write captions (sentences) under each picture to give the main points of the story.

Common story patterns

Many stories follow a similar pattern.

Introduction ➡ Build-up ➡ Climax ➡ Resolution

Write the resolution (ending) to Unit 1.1.
Think about:

◆ Who could the men be signalling to? Why?
◆ What does Catchpole do? Try to stop them?
  Give a warning?
◆ How does the story end?

Imagine you are Ninny. Write a good ending to Unit 1.5.
Think about:

◆ How do you feel now you are a slave?
  How are you treated?
◆ Do you escape? If so, how? What happens?
◆ Does Offa, your leader, return and rescue you?

Playscripts

Read Unit 1.2 again.

◆ Pay special attention to the layout.
◆ Write another scene.
◆ Set it out as a playscript.
◆ Imagine Dad and Amy make some cakes.
◆ They get in a mess and something terrible happens.

Imagine the conversation Papa had with his children at
lunch in Unit 1.3. Write it out as a playscript.

Turning stories into plays

Choose one of the following scenes from
Red Riding Hood:

a) Red Riding Hood meets the wolf in the forest.
b) The wolf goes to Grandma's cottage.
c) Red Riding Hood finds 'grandma' (the wolf!) in bed.
d) Red Riding Hood is saved by a woodcutter.

Write it as a playscript.

Write a playscript for a scene from another traditional or
well-known story.

Handy hints for playscripts

Characters

◆ Decide who the
  characters will be.
◆ Start a new line each
  time a new character
  speaks.
◆ Always write the name
  of the speaker clearly
  (see Units 1.2 and 1.4).

Set the scene

◆ Have a storyteller (or
  narrator) to do it or...
◆ Write an introduction
  (like Unit 1.4).

Instructions to actors

◆ Give instructions to
  actors in brackets.

How are you getting on with the things in the chart? If you need extra practice, try the activities shown.

Grammar and punctuation	Using verbs	1
	Verb tenses – past, present and future	2/3
	General punctuation	4
Spelling, phonics and vocabulary	Common letter strings	5
	Phonemes	6
	Verb past tenses ending with 'ed'	7
	Syllables	8
	Suffixes	9
	Spelling strategies	10

1 Copy these sentences. Underline the verbs in them.

I called for a friend. We went for a walk. I climbed a tree. My foot slipped and I fell down. I twisted my ankle badly. My friend ran home and told my Mum.

2 Rewrite the sentences in question 1. Change all the verbs into the future tense.

3 Change the verbs in these sentences into the past tense.

a) Some children play in the park.
b) My mum is baking a cake.
c) The gardener is digging his garden.
d) The police officer chases the robber.
e) The farmer ploughs the field.
f) Mrs Bell is watching television.
g) You are doing well.
h) It is a warm day.
i) I take the dog out.
j) The lion leaps at the impala.

4 Copy these sentences and put in the missing punctuation marks.

a) what time is it shouted Lucy
b) the builder shouted look out
c) can I come Emma asked
d) I dont know Sarah replied
e) the house with the broken window was empty
f) last night before going to bed Sam had a bath

5 *a)* Look at the words in Term 1 of the High Frequency Word List on page 96. Find as many words as you can containing the following letter strings:

ough   kn   ange   ear   atch   wr   ound   one   art

b) Now think of at least one more word containing each letter string. (Use a dictionary to check the spellings.)

c) Use the *Look, say, cover, write, check* method to learn the words.

6 For each word in Set A, find a word in Set B which has the same phoneme. Write the pairs of rhyming words in your book.

Set A

woke	shoe	fern	played	earth	brought	know

Set B

two	worth	go	fort	soak	fade	burn

7 Change these verbs into the past tense. They should all end in 'ed'.

Do it like this: try – tried

a) climb   *b)* try   *c)* drop   *d)* wash   *e)* plan   *f)* hurry
g) skid   *h)* kick   *i)* dry   *j)* stop   *k)* follow   *l)* study

8 Copy these words and break them into syllables like this: rabbit = rab – bit

a) cattle   *b)* sudden   *c)* passing   *d)* digger
e) stammer   *f)* follow   *g)* grabbing   *h)* bossy
i) happy   *j)* happen

9 Take the suffixes off these words. Write the root words.

a) appearance   *b)* encouragement   *c)* information
d) resistance   *e)* pressure   *f)* action   *g)* correction

0 *a)* Choose ten words you need to learn from the lists on page 96. Use the *Look, say, cover, write, check* method to help you learn them.

b) Make up some sentences and use the words in them.

Handy hints for spelling

◆ *Look* – Look carefully at the word.

◆ *Say* – Say the word to hear how it sounds.

◆ *Cover* – Cover the word and try to see it in your mind.

◆ *Write* – Write the word from memory.

◆ *Check* – Check your spelling with the original. Compare them.

Women's Talk

A woman's place is at the loom. Or is it?

A reporter from *The Greek News* talks to a woman from Rhodes, who has been married for ten years.

Question   Are you happy in your marriage?

Answer   Well, I do get a bit fed up sometimes. My whole life seems to be spent running the household – giving orders to the slaves or looking after the children.

I do envy my husband. He's often out working, or wining and dining. I can't do those things!

I never see anyone really. I stay in the women's quarters all the time. When my husband has friends around for dinner, I'm not allowed to join them.

Question   But you do get out of the house sometimes?

Answer   Only a few times a year, for religious festivals.

Question   But isn't running a home enough to keep any woman busy?

Answer   Women can do more than men think. There are women who manage jobs outside the home. Some work as market traders, while others help to deliver babies. There have been famous women poets, too, like Sappho.

Question   Do you think women should have more say in what goes on?

Answer   Well, men obviously don't think so! After all, we can't make speeches in the Assembly, or vote on any decisions they make there. I think they forget that some Greek cities have women rulers.

Question   Any last advice to young women?

Answer   Enjoy your girlhood – once you're married there'll be nothing but housework and children!

POTTY SALE

ONLY THE BEST FOR YOUR BABY! OUR CLAY POTTIES ARE STURDY AND COMFORTABLE – NO HOME SHOULD BE WITHOUT ONE.

The Pottery, next to the Theatre, Epidauros

From The Greek News *by Anton Powell and Philip Steale*

T

1 This piece from a newspaper is an interview. Explain what an interview is.
2 What does the headline tell you?
3 Who is the interview between?
4 Who is the article aimed at? Give your reasons.
5 Do you think this is from a modern or an ancient newspaper? Say why.
6 What is the interview mainly about?
7 List some of the reasons for the woman's unhappiness.
8 How is the interview set out? How helpful is this when you are reading it?
9 Why do you think there is an advertisement for babies' potties in the article?
10 List two facts and two opinions stated in the report.

NTENCE

1 Rewrite each sentence so that the verb agrees with the subject. The first is done for you.
  a) The woman do her work well. The woman does her work well.
  b) I gets a bit fed up. *c)* Some women works as market traders.
  d) There has been women poets. *e)* The reporter were asking questions.
  f) We was in the kitchen. *g)* She have given some answers.
  h) Each of the women were married. *i)* Don't he know anything?
2 Explain what the subject of a sentence is.
3 Copy and complete this rule and try to memorise it:
  The subject and v _ _ _ in each sentence must agree.

RD

1 Find each of the words below in the passage. Check their meanings in a dictionary and write a definition for each.
  whole friends allowed religious enough busy decisions advice young
2 Underline the trickiest bit of each word.
3 Use the *Look, say, cover, write, check* method of learning to spell the words.
4 Write the words in alphabetical order.
5 Add the suffix 'ing' to the verbs below, like this: dine – dining
  make hide poke tune fade smile owe cure face whine
6 Make up a rule explaining what you have discovered.

My Grandma's a Bank Robber!

MY GRANDMA'S A BANK ROBBER!

A 68-year-old grandma holding up a bank? Never? If you think it couldn't happen – read on!

Ivy Hammond is everyone's idea of a favourite grandma. She has grey hair tied up in a bun, wears a pink cardigan and carries a big, black handbag. She loves knitting and looking after her grandchildren. She wouldn't harm a fly – or would she? Ivy is currently in jail, serving a prison sentence for robbery.

Two months ago, Ivy, who lives in Worthing in Sussex, robbed a local bank. She put a stocking mask over her head, pretended she had a gun under a folded newspaper, and walked into the bank. She threatened the cashier and demanded money. The cashier gave her £100. Ivy, always so well-mannered, smiled, said, "Thank you", and left. The cashier called the police and they caught Ivy on the sea front buying an ice-cream!

Ivy told our reporter, "I got married when I was sixteen. All my life I've brought up children and looked after my home. I've had a happy life but I've never really done anything exciting. Now I'm famous. I've been on TV and in the newspapers." When asked if she would do it again, she smiled and said sweetly, "I think once is enough, don't you?"

Superintendent Smythe, of the Sussex police, said, "It's an unusual case. I have some sympathy for Mrs Hammond, but a crime is a crime and must be punished."

T

1 The newspaper report contains many facts. Read it and answer these questions:

a) What was the name of the woman? *b)* How old was she?

c) Describe her appearance. *d)* Where did she live?

e) What were her main interests? *f)* What crime did she commit?

2 How is the report set out – in lines across the page or in columns?

3 Is it set out as a block of text or in paragraphs?

4 What impression do you get of Mrs Hammond from the photograph?

5 In what way is the headline 'eye-catching'?

6 What do you think of the introduction to this report? Give your reasons.

7 Which two people does the reporter quote in the report?

ᴛENCE

1 In the newspaper report each paragraph is about something different. The first paragraph introduces the report. What are the other paragraphs mainly about?

2 The reporter also interviewed Mrs Hammond's grandson, Edward. Make up a paragraph about this and include a quote from the grandson.

3 Write and say what you think the headlines below could be about.

Cat makes Queen smile

RATS CLOSE SCHOOL!

Schoolgirl footballer tackles the England team

Locals protest over new road

ʀᴅ

1 Write a definition for each word. Use a dictionary to help if necessary.

cardigan mask pretend cashier sympathy punish

2 Find these words in the report. They can have more than one meaning.
Use each word in two different sentences to show the different meanings.

holding up bun sentence left case

3 Copy these sentences. Choose the correct homophone to fill in each gap.

a) The ____ children went ____ the park. Their mother went ____ . (too, two, to)

b) The children are going up to ____ bedroom. ____ going to bed. They will read
a book up ____ . (there, they're, their)

4 Write sentences to show the difference between these pairs of homophones:

brake, break   knew, new   threw, through   hear, here

23

Pet Poems

Peter's Pets

In his bedroom, Peter kept
TEN earwigs that scuttled and hid,
NINE spiders that wove their webs,
EIGHT white mice with pink little eyes,
SEVEN hamsters that snoozed in the cage,
SIX black cats, who were after the mice,
FIVE big dogs under the bed,
FOUR pigs, lazy and fat,
THREE pythons who hung from the light,
TWO donkeys who lived in the wardrobe,
and ONE ... GUESS WHAT?

David Orme

The Dog Lovers

So they bought you
And kept you in a
Very good home
Central heating
TV
A deep freeze
A very good home –
No one to take you
For that lovely long run –
But otherwise
'A very good home'.
They fed you Pal and Chum
But not that lovely long run,
Until, mad with energy and boredom
You escaped – and ran and ran and ran
Under a car.
Today they will cry for you –
Tomorrow they will buy another dog.

Spike Milligan

A Day in the Life of Danny the Cat

Danny wakes up
Eats
Finds a private place in the garden
He returns
Plays with the plants
And sleeps
Danny wakes up
Eats
Inspects the garden
Finds a cosy place
And sleeps
Danny wakes up
Comes indoors
Inspects the carpet
Scratches himself
And sleeps
Danny wakes up
Goes in the garden
Over the fence
Has a fight with Ginger
Makes a date with Sandy
Climbs on to next door's shed
And sleeps

Benjamin Zephaniah

T

1 Are the poems opposite about farm animals, pets or wild animals?

2 Which poem is: *a)* a sad poem   *b)* a poem about daily life   *c)* a counting poem?

3 Do any of the poems rhyme?

4 What do you notice about the way the poem about the cat is set out?

5 Why do you think the poet wrote the poem about the dog?

6 Which poem do you prefer? Say why.

7 Write a few more lines for the poem about the cat, in the same style.

8 Make up a poem about ten strange pets kept by an old lady. Set it out like *Peter's Pets*.

9 Find and read *a)* some more pet poems *b)* some poems about other animals
   c) some sad poems *d)* some more poems by Spike Milligan.

NTENCE

1 Copy these sentences and underline the adverb in each.

   a) The dog barked loudly.   *b)* The cat purred softly.   *c)* I ran home quickly.
   d) Quietly the thief opened the door.   *e)* The lady was dressed smartly.
   f) Always cross the road carefully.   *g)* A nurse smiled sweetly at the baby.
   h) Some ducks quack noisily.

2 Think of a good adverb to complete each of these sentences:

   a) The puppy ate his food _____ .   *b)* The giant laughed _____ .
   c) We finished the work _____ .   *d)* The bulldog growled _____ .
   e) It rained _____ .   *f)* I walked _____ across the road.
   g) I sat _____ in the dentist's chair.   *h)* The driver swerved _____ .

3 Think of as many different adverbs as possible to describe each of these verbs. Do it
   like this: You can run slowly, quickly, tiredly, breathlessly.

   a) How can you eat?   *b)* How can you talk?   *c)* How can you work?

RD

1 Match up the present tense of the verbs in Set A with the past tense in Set B.
   Write the pairs of verbs in your book, like this: break – broke

Set A	catch	fight	go	know	see	teach	write	eat	strike	can
Set B	fought	knew	struck	caught	wrote	went	saw	could	ate	taught

2 Make up some sentences. Use the past tense of the verbs in them.

25

Facts about Food – Britain

Eating in Britain can be quite an adventure!

Here are a few tips to help you.

Breakfast

A traditional English breakfast is a big meal and could include sausages, bacon, eggs, tomatoes, mushrooms and fried bread. This is filling and tasty! However, most people just have cereal and milk, or toast and marmalade (made from oranges) or jam (made from other fruits). People often drink fruit juice with breakfast. Most people drink either tea or coffee, both of which are served with cold milk. The coffee is usually instant coffee which tastes awful!

Lunch

For many people lunch is a quick meal. Over the last few years there has been a growth of fast-food places where you can get a quick, filling lunch, although the service in some of these places leaves a lot to be desired. Many people just have a sandwich. In big towns there are lots of sandwich bars, where you can get any sort of sandwich you want filled with salad, meat or fish. Pubs often serve good, cheap hot or cold snacks. School children can take a packed lunch with them or get a hot school dinner if they wish. School dinners are not very good on the whole.

Tea

This can mean two things. It can be a drink or a meal! Some people have a light afternoon tea, with sandwiches and cakes, and a cup of tea.

Evening meal

This is the main meal of the day for many people and is usually eaten between 6.00 and 8.00 pm. It is a time when the whole family may eat together. A favourite meal is fried fish and chips.

Sundays

The best British meal is the traditional Sunday lunch. This consists of roast meat with potatoes, vegetables and gravy. (Gravy is a sauce made from meat juices.)

International food

The British like food from other countries, especially Italy, France, China and India. People often get take-away meals from a restaurant and then bring them home to eat.

T

1 What is this article all about?

2 Which of these do you think it is written for: *a)* people coming to Britain on holiday *b)* people who already live in Britain? Give your reasons.

3 How many paragraphs does the article contain?

4 How can you tell what each paragraph is going to be about before you read it?

5 Find and write *a)* three facts stated in the article *b)* three opinions given.

6 Think of three other facts you would like to add.

7 Give your opinion of the traditional Sunday lunch.

8 How helpful is the article for vegetarians (people who do not eat meat)? Give your reasons.

ᴬTENCE

1 Copy the paragraph on 'Breakfast'. Underline all the verbs in it. Write a sentence saying whether the verbs are in the present or past tense.

2 Copy the paragraph below. Underline all the verbs in it. Write a sentence saying whether the verbs are in the present or past tense.

I showed him the gold chain around my neck. That was another mistake. He almost pulled my ears off as he stripped it from me.

3 Copy and complete this sentence and try to memorise it:

In stories verbs are usually in the _____ tense.

In non-fiction passages verbs are usually in the _____ tense.

4 Write a paragraph on each of the following topics: *a)* a fast-food hamburger restaurant *b)* a typical fish-and-chip shop *c)* a sandwich bar.

ᵂᴼᴿᴰ

1 Think up some funny sentences to help you remember how to spell these words. The first one is done to give you the idea.

a) sausages – It takes *ages* to cook sausages.

b) tomatoes   *c)* mushrooms
d) bread   *e)* cereal   *f)* sandwich
g) vegetable   *h)* breakfast
i) carrot   *j)* yoghurt   *k)* piece

2 Rewrite these sentences. Correct the spelling mistakes.

I like a big brekfast. I ofen eat sosages, tomatos and bred. Sometimes I also have sereal with millk, as well as sum tost and marmalaid. At lunchtimes I ushually only have a sanwich. My favorit evning meal is a rost dinner with lots of vegtables. For a change, I sometims have a tack-away meel.

Playing Conkers

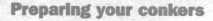

You need

- conkers (from horse chestnut trees)
- string
- vinegar

Preparing your conkers

Your conkers need to be hard.

1 Leave them in a warm, dry place for as long as possible to let them dry out and harden.
OR
Soak the conkers in vinegar overnight.

Then bake them in the oven for 30 mins.

(Ask a grown-up for help.)

2 Make a hole through each conker with something sharp. (Ask a grown-up for help.)

3 Thread the conker onto about half a metre of string, and tie a large knot so the conker will not fall off.

The Aim of the Game — To smash the conker of an opponent

Playing the game

- Players take turns to hit the opponent's conker (see diagram).
- Each person gets three shots at a time.
- The game finishes when one conker is smashed.

Scoring

- A conker may be called a 'oner' or a 'tenner', for example, depending on the number of conkers it has smashed.

- A new conker always starts off as a 'oner'.

- If it smashes another 'oner' it becomes a 'twoer'.

- If it smashes a 'fiver' it becomes a 'sixer' and so on.

T

1 What are the instructions opposite all about?

2 *a)* Are the instructions set out in one block of text or in sections? *b)* How does this help you? *c)* How can you tell what each section is going to be about?

3 What is the first section? Do you think it is a good idea to put this first? Say why.

4 How can you tell where to get conkers? How does the picture help you?

5 Why do you think the second section is numbered?

6 Are the pictures in the 'Playing the game' section helpful? Why?

7 Copy these instructions and underline the verbs:

   a) Leave the conkers in a warm place.   *b)* Soak the conkers in vinegar.
   c) Bake them in an oven.   *d)* Ask a grown-up for help.

8 Instructions sound strange if *you* are mentioned directly. Write the instructions in question 7 again, like this: You leave the conkers in a warm place.

9 Write a clear set of instructions for using a public telephone.

NTENCE

1 Copy the sentences. Complete each sentence with the most suitable adverb in the list.
angrily gracefully peacefully carefully easily neatly

   a) Read instructions _____ .   *b)* A swan swims _____ .
   c) You should write _____ .   *d)* The baby was sleeping _____ .

2 Rewrite each sentence. Use an adverb in the place of the underlined words.
Do it like this: Tom jumped two metres <u>with ease</u>. Tom jumped two metres easily.

   a) The vase was broken <u>by accident</u>.   *b)* The teacher left the room <u>in a hurry</u>.
   c) The man answered <u>in anger</u>.   *d)* I did it <u>straightaway</u>.

RD

1 Form an adverb from each adjective by adding the suffix 'ly', like this: slow – slowly.
quick glad narrow plain near cheap

2 Form an adverb from each adjective by adding the suffix 'ly', like this:
humble – humbly. **noble possible simple idle horrible gentle**

3 Write a sentence saying what you noticed in question 2.

4 Form an adverb from each adjective by adding the suffix 'ly', like this:
hungry – hungrily. **easy lucky angry heavy noisy weary**

5 Write a sentence saying what you noticed in question 4.

Do an interview

1 Imagine you are a reporter who interviews famous people.

- ◆ Choose who you are going to interview:
  - a famous sports person, pop singer, politician, etc.
  - someone that you know about from history.
- ◆ Think of four or five interesting questions you might ask.
- ◆ Work out what sort of answers the person might give.
- ◆ Write a report of your interview.
- ◆ Set it out like Unit 1.6.
  - Write a short paragraph for each answer.
  - Include a picture and a caption.

Write an article

2 Imagine you are writing an article in a magazine for people who are thinking of buying a pet. Choose a pet that you know something about, e.g. a dog, cat, etc.

a) Write a paragraph on each of the following:

- ◆ Food: what sort of things the pet eats and drinks, how often to feed it, etc.
- ◆ Things to buy: mention the things you would definitely need and why. For example, for a dog you would need things like a lead, a basket, etc.
- ◆ Keeping healthy and clean: does the pet need exercising, cleaning, etc.?
- ◆ Why have a pet? Mention some advantages (like being good company) and some disadvantages (like time, effort, cost, etc.).

b) Use Unit 1.9 to help you with layout:

- ◆ Think of a good title.
- ◆ Each section should consist of one paragraph.
- ◆ Give each section a clear heading.
- ◆ Add some interesting pictures.

Write a report

MY GRANDMA'S A BANK ROBBER!

'ye-catching'
eadline

icture or photo
nd caption

nteresting
ntroduction

lenty of facts

uotes (what
eople say)

et out in
aragraphs

A 68-year-old grandma holding up a bank? Never? If you think it couldn't happen – read on!

Ivy Hammond is everyone's idea of a favourite grandma. She has grey hair tied up in a bun, wears a pink cardigan and carries a big, black handbag. She loves knitting and looking after her grandchildren. She wouldn't harm a fly – or would she? Ivy is currently in jail, serving a prison sentence for robbery.

Two months ago, Ivy, who lives in Worthing in Sussex, robbed a local bank. She put a stocking mask over her head, pretended she had a gun under a folded newspaper, and walked into the bank. She threatened the cashier and demanded money. The cashier gave her £100. Ivy, always so well-mannered, smiled, said, "Thank you", and left. The cashier called the police and they caught Ivy on the sea front buying an ice-cream!

Ivy told our reporter, "I got married when I was sixteen. All my life I've brought up children and looked after my home. I've had a happy life but I've never really done anything exciting. Now I'm famous. I've been on TV and in the newspapers." When asked if she would do it again, she smiled and said sweetly, "I think once is enough, don't you?"

Superintendent Smythe, of the Sussex police, said, "It's an unusual case. I have some sympathy for Mrs Hammond, but a crime is a crime and must be punished."

Use the model above to help you write a report. Here are some ideas:

- Write about something that you have done, at home or school, somewhere you've visited or something exciting that has happened to you.
- Look again at Units 1 to 5. Turn these stories or plays into newspaper reports.
- Take any nursery rhyme, e.g. Humpty Dumpty, or well-known story, e.g. Jack and the Beanstalk, and rewrite them as newspaper or TV reports.
- ◆ Choose a newspaper headline. Make up your own report on what you think it will be about. Then read the original report and compare the two.
- Have fun making up reports about any of these headlines:

Fruit lorry spills load and makes a motorway jam!

The great escape

Terrible attack at castle

Handy hints on editing your work

Sentences

Do your sentences make sense? Is there anything you want to move or change? Is there anything you can leave out to make it clearer?

Punctuation

Have you punctuated it correctly with capital letters, full stops, question marks, exclamation marks and commas?

Spelling

Have you checked for silly spelling mistakes? Have you looked up any words you are not sure of?

Handwriting

Is your handwriting easy to read? Are you going to do your work on the computer?

LOOK
SAY
COVER
WRITE
CHECK

How are you getting on with the things in the chart? If you need extra practice, try the activities shown.

Grammar and punctuation	Subject and verb agreement	1
	Paragraphs	2
	Adverbs	3
Spelling, phonics and vocabulary	Spelling strategies	4 and 5
	Proofreading	6
	Suffixes	7 and 8
	Word definitions	9
	Homophones	10

1 Choose the correct form of each verb to ensure subject and verb agreement.

a) The children always _____ their bedroom. (tidy, tidies)

b) _____ the sky look beautiful today? (don't, doesn't)

c) All dogs_____ bones. (like, likes)

d) They _____ drinking noisily. (was, were)

e) Neither the boy nor the girl _____ asleep. (is, are)

2 Write a paragraph on what you know about each of the following:

a) crocodiles   *b)* monkeys   *c)* elephants

3 Copy the sentences. Underline the adverb in each.

a) The dog ate a bone greedily.

b) The birds sang sweetly in the trees.

c) The lady read her book quietly.

d) The children happily played in the sea.

e) The telephone rang noisily.

f) The car skidded wildly.

g) "Come quickly," I shouted.

h) I wrote my name neatly.

a) Copy these verbs carefully. Underline the tricky bit in each.

**built   burst   wrote   sprang   laid   broke   caught
crept   drowned   knew**

b) Use the *Look, say, cover, write, check* method for learning them.

c) Make up some sentences containing the words.

a) Choose ten words you need to learn from the Term 1 section on page 96. Use the *Look, say, cover, write, check* method to help you learn them.

b) Make up some sentences and use the words in them.

5 Copy these sentences. Proofread them and correct any spelling mistakes. Use a dictionary to check words if necessary.

In the feeld there were for rats with long tayls. A gray hors was standing by the fense. Som cows were graysing hapily, munching gras. The farmer opend the gate and came in with his tracter. His dog barkt and ran in ahed of him.

7 Add the suffix 'ing' to these verbs. Do it like this: decide – deciding

a) refuse   **b)** enclose   **c)** receive   **d)** waste
e) explore   **f)** whistle

8 Add the suffix 'ly' to these adjectives to make them into adverbs. Do it like this: slow – slowly

a) sudden   **b)** lazy   **c)** terrible   **d)** careful   **e)** clumsy
f) comfortable

9 Write a definition for each adjective below. Use a dictionary if necessary.

a) moist **b)** obstinate **c)** tranquil   **d)** amiable
e) rare   **f)** reluctant

Now make up some sentences containing each word.

10 Write sentences to show you know the difference between these homophones. Use a dictionary if you are not sure.

a) sail, sale   **b)** made, maid   **c)** stair, stare
d) allowed, aloud

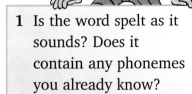

Handy hints for spelling

1 Is the word spelt as it sounds? Does it contain any phonemes you already know?

2 Does the word look right? Do you know any other words like it?

3 Can you break the word into smaller parts? Which is the most difficult part of the word?

4 Do you know what the word means?

5 Have you used a word book or dictionary to help you?

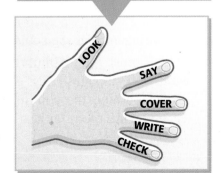

LOOK SAY COVER WRITE CHECK

Through the Wardrobe

Peter, Susan, Edmund and Lucy are in a strange house which they decide to explore. One room is completely empty except for a large wardrobe.

Lucy stayed behind because she thought it would be worth trying the door of the wardrobe, even though she felt almost sure it would be locked. To her surprise it opened quite easily, and two mothballs dropped out.

Looking into the inside, she saw several coats hanging up – mostly long fur coats. There was nothing Lucy liked as much as the smell and feel of fur. She immediately stepped into the wardrobe and got in among the coats and rubbed her face against them, leaving the door open, of course, because she knew that it is very foolish to shut oneself in any wardrobe. Soon she went further in and found that there was a second row of coats hanging up behind the first one. It was almost quite dark in there and she kept her arms stretched out in front of her so as not to bump her face into the back of the wardrobe. She took a step further in – then two or three steps – always expecting to feel woodwork against the tips of her fingers. But she could not feel it.

"This must be simply an enormous wardrobe!" thought Lucy, going still further in and pushing the soft folds of the coats aside to make room for her. Then she noticed there was something crunching under her feet. "I wonder if that's more mothballs?" she thought, stooping down to feel it with her hand. But instead of feeling the hard, smooth wood of the floor of the wardrobe, she felt something soft and powdery and extremely cold. "This is very queer," she said, and went on a step or two further.

Next moment she found that what was rubbing against her face and hands was no longer soft fur but something hard and rough and even prickly. "Why, it's just like branches of trees!" exclaimed Lucy. And then she saw that there was a light ahead of her; not a few inches away where the back of the wardrobe ought to have been, but a long way off. Something cold and soft was falling on her. A moment later she found that she was standing in the middle of a wood at night-time with snow under her feet and snowflakes falling through the air.

From The Lion, the Witch and the Wardrobe *by C.S. Lewis*

.T

1 *a)* Who is the main character in the passage? *b)* What does she explore?
c) What surprised her about the door of the wardrobe?

2 *a)* What does Lucy like about fur coats? *b)* What does she do to them?

3 *a)* What was it like by the second row of coats? *b)* What did Lucy do?
c) What surprised her?

4 Describe how Lucy realised she was touching a tree, not the wardrobe.

5 What words does the author use to tell you where Lucy found herself in the end?

6 *a)* How well do you think the author describes the setting?
b) Write two descriptions you particularly like.

7 What is *a)* the title of the book from which the passage came *b)* the name of the author? (This book is part of a series called the *Chronicles of Narnia*.
See if you can discover the titles of any other books in the series.)

TENCE

1 Copy and complete these sentences with different types of adjectives.
Do it like this: The elephant was <u>huge</u> but the flea was <u>tiny</u>. (size)

a) The giant was _____ but the mouse was _____ . (size)
b) China is a _____ way away but France is _____ . (distance)
c) Cotton wool feels _____ but stone feels _____ . (texture)
d) I have _____ legs but a cat has _____ legs. (number)

2 Find at least one of each of the following types of adjectives in the passage:

a) size   *b)* distance   *c)* texture   *d)* number   *e)* heat   *f)* colour

3 Copy and complete each phrase below with suitable adjectives:

a) a _____ , _____ hill   *b)* a _____ , _____ night
c) the _____ , _____ cat   *d)* some _____ , _____ apples

D

1 Write the pairs of words in the list below that have the same endings. Underline
the common letter string in each word. Do it like this: fur<u>ious</u>, obv<u>ious</u>.

enormous   special   possible   dangerous   official   sensible

2 Learn these words using the *Look, say, cover, write, check* method.

3 Choose one word from each pair. Write some sentences using the words you have chosen.

4 Think of at least one other word with the same word ending to go with each pair
of words you have written in question 1.

A Holiday on Earth

The Zome Kraft hissed through outer space and entered the solar system, left of the sun and right of the moon, where it altered course and began to slow down, spinning towards its destination.

"Commence Earth Approach!" ordered Mum Misty, crouching over the control panel.

"Commence Approach!" echoed Dad.

"Is that it?" asked Odle.

"What?"

"Earth," said Odle, and he bam-bam-bammed what he could see of it on the see screen with his space gun.

"That's Earth," said Dad. "Stay away from those launch buttons, Odle!"

"I'm hungry," little Mo announced.

"You're always hungry," said Odle.

"But I am," said Mo. "Isn't there anything to eat?"

"Zero 3900, descending," said Mum. "Give her a food block, somebody."

Dad gave Mo a food block. It was small, about the size of a chocolate bar, but it was packed with energy.

"Yummy!" said Mo, taking a big bite.

"I bet you'll be sick," said Odle.

"You make me sick!" said Mo.

"Not as sick as you'll be if old Two-Legger Earth Monster gets you," said Odle.

"Odle!" snapped Mum and Dad Misty together.

"Are there many Earth Monsters, Mum?" Mo asked nervously.

"Lots!" said Odle. "There are Flappers that fly and Finners that swim and Roarers that roar in the jungle and horrible Two-Leggers and ..."

"They're all very small, Mo dear," said Mum, quickly. "You know that."

"Will they eat me?" asked Mo, finishing the last bite of her food block.

"No," said Mum.

"Yes!" said Odle.

"ODLE!" said Dad.

From Blue Misty Monsters *by Catherine Sefton*

1 a) Where does the passage take place (its setting)? b) Is it in the present or the future? c) What is the spacecraft called? d) Where was it going?

2 a) List the parts of the spacecraft that are mentioned.
b) What is Odle carrying? c) What kind of food does the family eat?

3 a) What are the names of the space travellers? b) Why are they travelling to Earth? How do you know? c) How can you tell Mo has never been before?
d) How do you know that they do not look like us (i.e. humans)?

4 a) Who is older – Mo or Odle? Say how you know.
b) How does Odle treat Mo? How can you tell?

5 What sort of monster do you think each of the following is:
a) a Two-Legger   b) a Flapper   c) a Finner   d) a Roarer?

6 Often writers use similes to describe things, e.g. The Earth was like a big ball.
Copy and complete these similes with suitable words:
a) as dry as a _____   b) as bright as _____
c) as sweet as _____   d) The smooth sea was like _____ .

7 Do you think this story is aimed at a) young children b) children between the ages of 7 and 11 c) older teenagers or adults? Give your reasons.

TENCE

1 Copy this sentence. Fill in the gaps with suitable nouns.
The _____ _____ entered the _____ _____ , left of the
_____ and right of the _____ .

2 Copy and complete this definition: A noun is a _____ word.

3 Copy these sentences. Underline the adjectives in them.
The monster was scary. It had a round head with wavy hair and huge eyes. Its mouth was full of sharp teeth. It spoke a strange language in a loud voice.

4 Write at least one synonym for each adjective you have written. Use a dictionary or thesaurus to help if necessary. Do it like this: scary – frightening.

5 Explain what a synonym is.

RD

1 How many small words can you find in each of the compound words below?
spacecraft   butterfly   snowflake   earthquake   together   grandmother

2 Learn these words using the *Look, say, cover, write, check* method.

3 Make up some sentences and use the words in them.

37

A Mad Tea Party

Alice had drunk a magic potion which had made her very small. It enabled her to enter Wonderland, where nothing was ever quite what it seemed!

There was a table set out under a tree in front of the house, and the March Hare and the Hatter were having tea at it. A Dormouse was sitting between them, fast asleep. The table was a large one, but the three were all crowded together at one corner of it. "No room! No room!" they cried out when they saw Alice coming. "There's plenty of room," said Alice indignantly, and she sat down in a large armchair at one corner of the table.

"Have some wine," the March Hare said in an encouraging tone.

Alice looked round the table, but there was nothing on it but tea. "I don't see any wine," she remarked.

"There isn't any," said the March Hare.

"Then it wasn't very civil of you to offer it," said Alice angrily.

"It wasn't very civil of you to sit down without being invited," said the March Hare.

"I didn't know it was *your* table," said Alice. "It's laid for a great many more than three."

"Your hair wants cutting," said the Hatter. He had been looking at Alice for some time with great curiosity, and this was his first speech.

"You should learn not to make personal remarks," Alice said, with some severity. "It's very rude."

The Hatter opened his eyes very wide on hearing this; but all he said was, "Why is a raven like a writing-desk?"

"Come, we shall have some fun now!" thought Alice. "I'm glad they've begun asking riddles – I believe I can guess that," she added aloud.

"Do you mean you think you can find the answer for it?" asked the March Hare.

"Exactly so," said Alice.

"Then you should say what you mean," the March Hare went on.

"I do," Alice hastily replied. "At least – at least I mean what I say – that's the same thing, you know."

"Not the same thing a bit!" said the Hatter. "Why, you might just as well say that 'I see what I eat' is the same thing as 'I eat what I see'!"

"You might just as well say," added the March Hare, "that 'I like what I get' is the same thing as 'I get what I like'!"

"You might just as well say," added the Dormouse, who seemed to be talking in his sleep, "that 'I breathe when I sleep' is the same thing as 'I sleep when I breathe'!"

"It is the same thing with you," said the Hatter, and here the conversation dropped, and the party sat silent for a minute, while Alice thought over all she could remember about ravens and writing-desks, which wasn't much.

The Hatter took his watch out of his pocket, and looked at it uneasily, shook it, and held it to his ear. Then he dipped it in his cup of tea, and looked at it again.

From
Alice in Wonderland
by Lewis Carroll

1 *a)* How did Alice shrink? *b)* Where did she go? *c)* Who did she meet?

2 *a)* What was the first thing said to Alice? *b)* Why did she think this was odd?

3 *a)* What did the March Hare offer Alice? *b)* Why did she get angry?

4 What did the Hatter say to Alice that made her angry?

5 What was strange about the Dormouse?

6 What odd thing did the Hatter do at the end of the passage?

7 What do you think Alice made of the tea party and the other characters?

8 Explain how Units 2.1, 2.2 and 2.3 all involve going into unknown places.

9 Which of the three passages did you enjoy most? Say what you particularly liked about it. Would you recommend the story to a friend? Say why.

TENCE

1 Some words in the sentences below are in the wrong order. Rewrite them so they make sense, like this: The hole ran into the rabbit. The rabbit ran into the hole.
a) The chair sat on the man. *b)* The window washing the lady is.
c) I kick and run the ball. *d)* I stopped barking the dog.

2 Underline the verbs in the sentences you have written. At the end of each sentence write if the verb is in the present, past or future tense.

3 Explain how each sentence in these pairs of sentences has a different meaning.
a) I say what I mean. I mean what I say.   *b)* I see what I eat. I eat what I see.
c) I like what I get. I get what I like.
d) I breathe when I sleep. I sleep when I breathe.

D

1 Copy these words carefully:
potion   attractive   punishment   doctor   colour

2 Write a definition for each, using as few words as possible. (Use a dictionary if necessary.)

3 For each word, think of another one that has the same ending.

4 Now write all your ten words in alphabetical order.

5 *a)* Write the plural of these words, like this: half – halves.
   half   calf   shelf   leaf   thief   loaf

   b) Write a sentence saying what you notice.

Sugarcane

When I take
a piece of sugarcane
and put it in me mouth
I does suck and suck
till all the juice come out.

I don't care
if is sun or rain
I does suck and suck
till all the juice come out.

But when I doing homewuk
and same time playing bout
Granny does tell me,
"How can you work
properly and play at
the same time?
You brain can't settle.
I always telling you
you can't suck cane
and whistle,
you can't suck cane
and whistle!"

John Agard

T

1 *a)* What does the girl like sucking? *b)* Why do you think this is?
c) Do you think sugarcane grows in Britain?

2 What makes you think Granny lives in the same house?

3 What do you think Granny means when she tells the girl that her brain 'can't settle' when she's playing about and trying to do her homework?

4 What does Granny mean when she says 'you can't suck cane and whistle'?

5 *a)* How many verses does this poem have? *b)* Is it a rhyming poem?

6 What clues are there in the poem that it is not set in Britain?

7 The poet writes in English but sometimes says things a little differently.
a) Find three examples of this in the poem.
b) Write how you would say each of these.

8 See if you can find any other poems by John Agard.

NTENCE

1 We can use comparative adjectives to describe things:
Pete had a long beard. Bert's beard was longer. Jim had the longest beard.
Compare the adjectives below. Do it like this: long – longer – longest.
a) small, bright, smooth, narrow *b)* large, brave, wise, safe
c) heavy, busy, noisy, tidy *d)* thin, hot, fat, big

2 Write a rule, saying what you discovered about the spelling of each set of adjectives.

3 When we compare longer adjectives, we have to use the words 'more' or 'most' in front of them, e.g. My cakes are delicious but yours are more delicious. Sam's cakes are the most delicious of all. Compare the adjectives below. Do it like this: delicious – more delicious – most delicious.
beautiful   honest   foolish   comfortable   famous   difficult   brilliant   powerful

R D

1 Divide the words below into syllables, like this: fan – tas – tic.
fantastic   important   homework   settle   Granny   telling   morning   suddenly

2 Write some sentences using the words in question 1.

3 We can make some comparative adjectives by adding the suffix 'ish' to words.
Add the suffix 'ish' to these adjectives, like this: long – longish.
brown   small   bright   thin   old   young   red   hard   soft   fat   wet   cold

41

The Lamplighter

My tea is nearly ready
    and the sun has left the sky;
It's time to take the window
    to see Leerie going by;
For every night at tea time
    and before you take your seat,
With lantern and with ladder
    he comes posting up the street.

Now Tom would be a driver
    and Maria go to sea,
And my papa's a banker
    and as rich as he can be;
But I, when I am stronger
    and can choose what I'm to do,
O Leerie, I'll go round at night
    and light the lamps with you!

For we are very lucky,
    with a lamp before the door,
And Leerie stops to light it
    as he lights so many more;
And O! before you hurry by
    with ladder and with light,
O Leerie, see a little child
    and nod to him tonight!

Robert Louis Stevenson

T

1 *a)* What time of day is it? How do you know? *b)* Has the child had tea yet?

2 *a)* Does the child come from a rich or a poor family?
   b) What does the child want to be when he or she grows up?

3 *a)* What is the name of the man the child is looking out for? *b)* What is his job?
   c) Do you think the man ever notices the child? Give your reasons.

4 *a)* How can you tell this poem is set in olden times? *b)* Write what you think each
   of these expressions means: *i)* It's time to take the window *ii)* before you take your
   seat *iii)* he comes posting up the street *iv)* a lamp before the door.

5 *a)* How many verses does the poem have? *b)* How many lines are there in each verse?
   c) Is it a rhyming poem? *d)* Does every line rhyme? *e)* Which lines do rhyme?

6 Write a review of the poem. Write: *a)* its title *b)* the name of the poet
   c) what it is about *d)* something you liked or disliked about it.

7 Find the names of some other poems or books written by Robert Louis Stevenson.

NTENCE

1 Copy these comparative adjectives into your book:
   a) good – better – best *b)* bad – worse – worst *c)* little – less – least

2 Write these sentences in order, according to the order of importance of the
   adjectives. Underline the adjectives in them:
   a) My book is best. Sam's book is good. Ben's book is better.
   b) My spellings were worse. Jan's spellings were the worst. Ali's spellings were bad.
   c) I had the least money. Alice had a little money. Will had less money than Alice.

3 Write these words in order. Say whether they are nouns, verbs or adjectives.
   a) minute, week, second, day, hour *b)* sentence, letter, paragraph, word, chapter

RD

1 Each of the adjectives below has a suffix. Write the noun from which each adjective
   comes. Do it like this: dangerous – danger.
   hungry poetic sunny childish noisy metallic gigantic foolish boyish

2 Now write the adjectives in question 1 above in three sets according to their suffixes.

3 Make adjectives from these nouns. Use the suffixes 'al', 'ous' and 'able'.
   Do it like this: music – musical.
   music mystery comfort favour fame accident fashion poison

4 Choose six of the adjectives you made in question 3 above. Make up some
   sentences of your own and include each of the adjectives you have chosen.

Setting the scene

Through the Wardrobe

1 Read Unit 2.1 again. Imagine you are Lucy.

- ◆ You find yourself in a wood at night. It is snowing.
- ◆ What sort of things do you think?
- ◆ Use interesting language and make it come alive!

- ◆ What do you see, hear, touch, smell?
- ◆ How do you feel?
- ◆ Write a description of the place.

The Misty Family Arrive on Earth

2 Read Unit 2.2 again. Imagine you are one of the Misty children on the Zome Kraft. You have never been to Earth before. Write your impressions of the place where you land. Include some good adjectives in your description. Choose one of the following places to land.

- ◆ the countryside
- ◆ a busy high street
- ◆ a theme park.

Alice's Walk in the Garden

3 Read Unit 2.3 again. In it Alice shrank.

- ◆ Imagine how strange things would seem if you were tiny.
- ◆ Write about going for a walk in the garden while you are small.
- ◆ Describe what you see and hear.
- ◆ Try to use some similes in your writing. (Look at the examples of similes on the right.)

There's a deafening, buzzing drone above, like ten angry aeroplanes – a bee!

A slug glides by, like a huge slimy monster, leaving a slippery trail.

Writing a longer story

◆ Develop one of the ideas from Setting the scene into a longer story.

◆ Plan your story in three chapters:

Chapter 1 Use the setting you wrote as the basis for your first chapter.

Chapter 2 Think of something exciting that could happen to you.

Chapter 3 Consider how the problem might be solved. Think of a good ending.

◆ Make sure:

– there is plenty of action and there are no boring parts.

– you describe the characters (what they look like, think, say, do).

– you describe the settings with colourful language.

◆ Write your story in rough first.

◆ Use the Handy hints on reviewing your work to help you make a finished version.

Some other ideas for stories

Writing for young children

◆ Make a picture book of Alice's Walk in the Garden for younger children.

◆ Write just a short sentence under each picture.

◆ Design a colourful cover.

◆ Read your story to the children.

Time Travellers

Imagine the Zome Kraft could travel backwards or forwards in time.

◆ Write a longer story of some of your adventures.

◆ Each chapter could be about a different visit in a different time setting.

Handy hints on reviewing your work

Making sense

Does your story make sense?
Can you add or move anything?
Can you leave anything out to make it clearer?
Is the punctuation right?

Language

Have you used interesting describing words?
Can you use any better words in places?
Have you checked for silly spelling mistakes?

Presentation

Will your work be illustrated?
Will you use a computer?
Will it be made into a book or other format?

How are you getting on with the things in the chart? If you need extra practice, try the activities shown.

Grammar and punctuation	Selecting suitable adjectives	1 and 2
	Types of adjectives	3
	Comparative adjectives	4
	Word order in sentences	5
Spelling, phonics and vocabulary	Spelling strategies	6 and 7
	Alphabetical order	8
	Common word endings	9
	Suffixes	10

1 Copy the sentences. Think of a suitable adjective for each gap.

a) The _____ cat was asleep on the _____ chair.

b) The _____ dragon came out of the _____ cave.

c) The _____ children picked some _____ apples.

d) A _____ boat was floating on the _____ sea.

2 Think of suitable adjectives to complete each phrase.

a) a _____ , _____ beggar

b) the _____ , _____ giant

c) a _____ , _____ banana

d) some _____ , _____ clothes

3 Copy these words and join the opposites.
Write which type of adjective each pair is like this:
sad – happy → feeling adjectives.

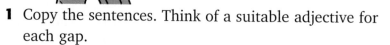

sad	sour	tall	near	light
sweet	happy	heavy	short	far

4 Compare these adjectives. Do it like this:
big – bigger – biggest

a) rough   *b)* slow   *c)* rude   *d)* wide   *e)* noisy

5 Re-order the words into sentences that make sense.

a) The small fish ate the shark.

b) The horse jumped on the jockey.

c) England is in London.

d) The egg is frying the lady.

e) Small eggs in the seven nest were there.

f) Wall car into the crashed a.

6 a) Find and write all the words with two syllables from the word list (Term 2) on page 96.

b) Use the *Look, say, cover, write, check* method to help you learn them.

c) Make up some sentences and use the words in them.

7 Copy these words carefully. Find the small words hiding in each.

Do it like this: bright – right

bright	**horrible**
system	**nothing**
crouching	**wardrobe**
space	**passage**
chocolate	**because**

8 Now rewrite the words in question 7 in alphabetical order.

9 Write these words in pairs according to their endings.

**appearance   satisfaction   boredom
punishment   freedom   excitement
resistance   conversation**

0 Choose the correct suffix to complete each word:

ish   y   ly   ous   ful   al

a) music _____   b) girl _____   c) wonder _____

d) sudden _____   e) danger _____   f) water _____

Handy hints for spelling

1 Is the word spelt as it sounds? Does it contain any phonemes you already know?

2 Does the word look right? Do you know any other words like it?

3 Can you break the word into smaller parts? Which is the most difficult part of the word?

4 Do you know what the word means?

5 Have you used a word book or dictionary to help you?

LOOK
SAY
COVER
WRITE
CHECK

The Clock Strikes Thirteen!

When Tom heard the old grandfather clock downstairs strike thirteen he went down to investigate.

Tom's attention was distracted by the opening of a door down the hall – the door of the ground-floor flat. A maid trotted out. Tom had seen housemaids only in pictures, but he recognised the white apron, cap and cuffs, and the black stockings. (He was not expert in fashions, but the dress seemed to him to be rather long for her.) She was carrying paper, kindling wood and a box of matches.

He had only a second in which to observe these things. Then he realised he ought to take cover at once; and there was no cover to take. Since he must be seen, Tom determined to be the first to speak – to explain himself. He did not feel afraid of the maid: as she came nearer he saw that she was only a girl. To warn her of his presence without startling her, Tom gave a cough; but she did not seem to hear it. She came on. Tom moved forward into her line of vision; she looked at him, but looked through him too, as though he were not there. Tom's heart jumped in a way he did not understand. She was passing him.

"I say!" he protested loudly; but she paid not the slightest attention. She passed him, reached the front door of the ground-floor flat, turned the door handle and went in. There was no bell-ringing or unlocking of the door.

Tom looked down and saw that he was standing on a rug – a tiger-skin rug. There were other rugs down the hall. His eyes now took in the rest of the hall – a hall that was different. No laundry box, no milk bottles, no travel posters on the walls. The walls were decorated with a rich variety of other objects instead: a tall Gothic barometer, a fan of peacock feathers, a huge engraving of a battle (hussars and horses and shot-riddled banners) and many other pictures. There was a big dinner gong, with its wash-leathered gong-stick hanging beside it. There was a large umbrella stand holding umbrellas and walking sticks and a parasol and an air-gun and what looked like parts of a fishing rod.

In that crowded hall, the only object Tom recognised was the grandfather clock. He moved towards it, not to read its face, but simply to touch it – to reassure himself that this at least was as he knew it. His hand was nearly upon it, when he heard a little breath behind him that was the parlour maid passing back the way she had come. For some reason, she did not seem to make as much sound as before. He heard her call only faintly, "I've lit the fire in the parlour."

She was making for the door through which she had first come, and, as Tom followed her with his eyes, he received a curious impression: she reached the door, her hand was on the knob, and then she seemed to go. That was it exactly: she went, but not through the door. She simply thinned out and went.

From Tom's Midnight Garden *by Phillipa Pearce*

T

1 *a)* What is the name of the boy? *b)* What made him go downstairs?

2 List some of the evidence Tom found that told him he had gone back in time.

3 *a)* Describe what was strange about the way the maid was dressed.

   b) How did Tom feel when he first saw the maid?

   c) What was odd about the way she looked at him?

   d) What do you think the author meant by 'she simply thinned out and went'?

4 *a)* What was the only thing Tom recognised in the hall?

   b) What was different about the hall?

5 How is the plot of this story similar to that of Units 2.2 and 2.3?

6 *a)* Who is the author? *b)* Can you find the names of any other stories by her?

NTENCE

1 Write these phrases a shorter way, using an apostrophe. Do it like this:
   the apron belonging to the maid – the maid's apron.
   a) The pen belonging to the boy *b)* The bag belonging to Tom
   c) The heart belonging to Tom *d)* The tail of the monkey

2 Say if the owner of each object in question 1 is singular or plural.

3 Write these without an apostrophe, e.g. the tiger's head – the head of the tiger.
   a) The woman's hat *b)* The teacher's book *c)* The car's headlight *d)* Sam's friend

4 Say if the owner of each object in question 3 is singular or plural.

5 Make up a rule for using an apostrophe when the object belongs to only one owner.

6 Write the longer form of the contractions below, like this: don't = do not.
   can't isn't wouldn't they're we'll I've

7 Write a sentence explaining why we use apostrophes as in question 6.

R D

1 List some of the nouns in the passage that are old-fashioned, e.g. parlour.
   Use a dictionary. Write a definition for each in as few words as possible.

2 Copy these words and say whether each is masculine (M) or feminine (F).
   Do it like this: princess (F).
   prince countess emperor princess duke duchess count goddess

3 *a)* Now write the nouns in question 2 in pairs. *b)* Say what you notice.

4 Write the feminine of these nouns, like this: son (M) – daughter (F).
   man boy son uncle father nephew lord brother husband

My Future

1 What will be
Left here for me
When I grow up?

2 Will there be
Pure air to breathe?
Will the sea be clean?

3 Will tarmac
Cover all the fields?
Will they still be green?

4 Milk from cows
Meat, veg and fruit
Will they be fit to eat?

5 Will sunlight hurt
Will fumes from cars
Clog up a crowded street?

6 Will blue whales sing?
Will elephants
and rhinos still survive?

7 Will you have left
Us anything
Healthy and alive?

8 When I've grown up
And I'm in charge
What will it be worth

9 If you have used
The goodness up
And destroyed the Earth?

David Harmer

T

1 *a)* What is the title of the poem? *b)* Who wrote it?
c) Is it a poem about the past, present or future?

2 Copy verse 2. Underline all the words used to create a positive feeling.

3 What is the poet really worried about?

4 Does the poet succeed in making you think? How does he do this?

5 Say something you like, or do not like, about the poem.

6 *a)* How many verses are there? *b)* How many lines are there in each verse?
c) Are there any choruses? *d)* Which lines rhyme in verses 2 and 3?

7 Find other poems with a similar theme, i.e. conservation and pollution.

NTENCE

1 Choose which of the adverbs below is best in front of each adjective:

very   really   most   quite

a) In the Arctic it is _____ cold. *b)* When I saw the ghost I was _____ scared.
c) I felt _____ tired. *d)* It was the _____ boring lesson ever!

2 Write the meaning of the phrases below, like this: the doctors' surgery – the surgery belonging to the doctors. (Note the position of the apostrophe when there is more than one owner, i.e. in the plural, and when their name ends in 's'.)
a) the cows' milk *b)* the monkeys' bananas *c)* the books' covers *d)* the girls' teeth

3 Write the difference between the phrases below:
a) the boy's boots; the boys' boots *b)* the girls' teacher; the girl's teacher
c) the pirates' gold; the pirate's gold *d)* the lady's bags; the ladies' bags

R D

1 Replace the underlined words with more interesting ones:
a) 'Stop thief!' <u>I said</u>. *b)* It was a <u>nice</u> day. *c)* I <u>got</u> the dress from a shop.
d) We had a <u>good</u> night at the circus. *e)* It was <u>nice</u> to see my long-lost uncle.

2 *a)* Write these words in alphabetical order:

always   already   almost   almighty   also   alone   although

b) What do you notice about the spelling of the prefix?

3 *a)* Write these words in alphabetical order:

awful   wonderful   helpful   useful   cheerful   beautiful

b) What do you notice about the spelling of the suffix?

Health and Beauty

Contents

Introduction	4
Food	6
Cloth	10
Buildings	12
Crafts	20
Transport	30
Warfare	34
Writing and Painting	36
Health and Beauty	40
The Afterlife	42
Technology through Time	44
Glossary	46
Further Information	47
Index	48

Smelling sweet

In this painting, the women have cones of perfumed animal fat on top of their party wigs. They probably did not really wear these – it is the artist's way of showing that they smelled strongly of perfume.

Making wigs

All Egyptians kept their hair short, cutting it with knives; scissors were not invented until after 100 BC. Those who could afford them wore wigs on special occasions. The wigs, like this one, were made of human hair, tied in strands onto a woven net.

Making medicines

Through their experiments, Egyptian doctors discovered that many plants and foods could be used to treat sickness and injury. They used willow leaves to soothe inflammation. These leaves contain salicylic acid – a chemical that we still use today in the form of aspirin. They used liver, which contains vitamin A, to heal sore eyes. Copper salts, which have a drying effect, were used to dry up wounds.

From Technology in Ancient Egypt *by Judith Croshe*

T

1 *a)* What book is the page opposite taken from? *b)* Where would you find the page in the book? *c)* On what pages of the book would you find information on: transport, writing and Egyptian gods?

2 What three topics does the page opposite cover?

3 *a)* Which of the following features describes the way the page is organised?

    lists   pictures   paragraphs   charts   diagrams   clear headings

  b) Is it easy to find your way about the page? Why?

4 How useful would this page be if you wanted to find out the information below?

  a) which Egyptians wore wigs *b)* how the Egyptian doctors dealt with broken legs
  c) whether Egyptians wore perfume *d)* what medicines the Egyptians used

5 Here are the main points one child wrote after reading the section on wigs:

Egyptians cut their hair short with knives. Scissors weren't invented.
Wealthy people sometimes wore wigs.

Write what you think are the main points of the other two paragraphs.

NTENCE

1 Copy these sentences and put in the missing commas.

  a) On the page opposite there are three topics.
  b) All Egyptians wore their hair short cutting it with knives.
  c) The wigs like the one in the picture were made of human hair.

2 Explain why we use commas in punctuation.

3 Copy these sentences. Underline the connectives in them, like this:
The Egyptians cut their hair short <u>so that</u> they would not get too hot.

  a) The Egyptian doctors studied plants in order to find cures for illnesses.
  b) Egyptian ladies wore perfume in case they smelt!

RD

1 Rewrite these sentences. Correct any spelling mistakes. Check the page opposite for words if you are unsure, or use a dictionary.

Egyptun wimen wore perfoomed aminal fat on there party wigs in order to smell nice. Most Egyptions kept they're hair short, by cutting it with knifes. Sissers were not inventd untill later. Some peple wore wigs made of humun hair.

2 Find all the words opposite that have a double consonant in them. Underline it. Say how many syllables each word contains. Do it like this: wi<u>ll</u>ow (2 syllables).

Farming in Ancient Egypt

The most important business in Egypt was farming. Most of the people were peasants, who worked all day in fields and barns.

The main food crops were wheat and barley, but many vegetables and some fruits were grown in gardens. Seed was sown after the flood waters had gone down. Crops had to be watered with the help of canals and ditches. Cattle, sheep and goats gave meat and milk. Some people kept ducks and pigeons but chickens were unknown.

During the flood season, when no farming could be done, peasants did building work on temples and palaces.

HARVEST
When the main crops were ready, nearly everyone – men, women, even priests – helped with the harvest.

TAXES
Farmers paid part of their crops as taxes. Scribes kept careful record of the amounts.

✓ **LOOK OUT FOR THESE**

☐ **SHADUF**
The shaduf was used to raise water. A pole was balanced on a pivot with a weight at one end and a bucket at the other. The weight made it easy to pull up water from a river or a well.

☐ **SICKLE**
Men cut the stalks of corn with a sickle. Modern sickles are much the same shape, but this one is wooden and has teeth of flint. It was used like a saw.

☐ **FLAX**
Flax is an annual plant with blue flowers. Fibres from the stem are used to make linen thread. Nearly all clothes were linen.

T

1 *a)* What is the page opposite about? *b)* What is the title of the book from which it came? *c)* What does this book have in common with the book used in Unit 2.8?

2 How does the page opposite differ in its organisation and presentation of information from the book shown in Unit 2.8?

3 What do you think is the purpose of
a) the labelled pictures and *b)* the 'Look out for these' section?

4 Think of a suitable heading for each paragraph opposite. For example, the first paragraph could be called 'The importance of farming'.

5 Explain what you like, or don't like, about the layout of the page.

6 List some of the ways that non-fiction books are different from fiction books. For example, non-fiction give information; fiction usually contain stories.

NTENCE

1 A child copied some information from the book but put in some wrong words, making the information inaccurate. Check the notes and write them correctly.

The most important farming in Egypt was business. Most of the peasants were people. Some vegetables and many fruits were grown in gardens. Seeds were sown before the flood waters had gone down. Cattle had to be watered with the help of canals. Wheat and barley gave meat and milk. Ducks were unknown in Egypt at this time. During the farming season, peasants did building work.

2 Put the words in the correct order and write them as proper sentences.

a) worked The fields. peasants the day all in
b) many grew The vegetables. Egyptians
c) canals. the obtained for Water crops was from
d) Some ducks people and pigeons. kept

RD

1 Find words in the passage containing these letter strings:
a) ear   *b)* eat   *c)* ead   *d)* ort   *e)* ork   *f)* ord   *g)* alk   *h)* ard   *i)* arm
j) arl   *k)* ood   *l)* tch   *m)* own   *n)* ght   *o)* ui   *p)* ttle   *q)* ace   *r)* are
s) ount   *t)* ance   *u)* ape   *v)* ckle   *w)* ould   *x)* ave   *y)* able   *z)* ole

2 Think of another word containing the same letter string as each word that you found in question 1.

Finding Your Way Around an Information Book

Here are the contents page and parts of the glossary and the index from a book about Ancient Egypt.

CONTENTS

GLOSSARY

Abu Simbel A place in Upper Egypt where two temples were moved to a new site to escape flooding in 1967.

Alexander the Great A Greek king who conquered Egypt and other lands in the 4th century BC.

amulet A magic charm.

Amun Amun became the chief god of the New Kingdom and was called 'King of the gods'.

Ankh A symbol meaning 'life'. It was carried by gods and kings.

Assyria A kingdom in Mesopotamia, which conquered Egypt in the 7th century BC.

Aswan A town near the first cataract (falls) of the Nile. It marked the boundary between Egypt and Nubia.

INDEX

From Spotlights – The Egyptians *by Neil Grant*

1 Which section of the book would you look in to find the page from Unit 2.9?

2 Look at the Contents Page. On which page do each of these sections begin:

a) Pharaohs *b)* Craftsmen *c)* Food and Drink *d)* Religion *e)* Family Life?

3 *a)* In which part of a book would you find *i)* the Contents Page *ii)* the Index? *b)* What is the difference between the two pages?

4 Look at the section from the Index. On which page would you find information on *a)* chariots *b)* beer *c)* the Aswan Dam *d)* clothes *e)* brushes *f)* board games *g)* amulets?

5 Which of the sections opposite are in alphabetical order? Why is this helpful?

6 What is the purpose of a glossary?

7 Use the Glossary to find the meaning of: *a)* amulet *b)* Amun *c)* Aswan.

TENCE

1 Write the plural of these nouns:

man woman child mouse

2 Write the meaning of these phrases: *a)* the women's voices *b)* the men's uniforms *c)* the children's books *d)* the mice's tails

3 Copy these sentences and punctuate them correctly.

a) the childrens shouts could be heard a long way away
b) the girls mother shouted give me that at once no I wont the little girl replied
c) who is that player the one wearing the muddy red shirt
d) oh cried the little boy Ive hurt my leg

D

1 Copy these words. Underline the root word in each one. Do it like this: dis<u>like</u>.

**helpful colourless comfortably methodical watery
information hopefully assistance pressure delivery**

2 Write the root word from which each of these words grew. Do it like this: satisfaction – satisfy.

**imagination arrival explosion marriage service circular
furious angry central energetic**

3 Think of a longer word that comes from each of the following root words.

help wash appear cover danger expense fright beauty begin

Notes

1 This diary entry is written in note form. Write it again in proper sentences. Do it like this: The noise of the birds woke me at 6 o'clock.

Noisy birds 6 a.m. Breakfast 7.30 – cereals, toast. a.m. Town – shopping – new trainers. Lunch – hamburger. p.m. walk in woods. Saw red fox and cubs. Rained. Soaked! Home to change. Read book. Uncle Bob to dinner. Watched TV evening. Boring. Bath and bed 9 p.m. (Read till 10.30!)

Diagrams

2 ◆ Look at the diagram and read the information. The diagram is numbered 1 to 5 but the names of the parts of the body have not been filled in yet. Use the information in the notes to help you decide how you would label this picture. Write the numbers 1 to 5 in your books and write the correct word next to it.

Notes

Your rib cage protects important parts of your body like your lungs and your heart. The hard bone of your skull protects your brain inside, which is very soft.

◆ Draw labelled diagrams showing the important parts of: *a)* the eye *b)* the ear

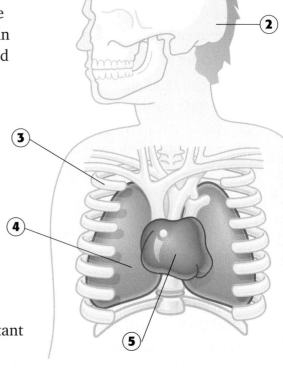

Explaining things clearly

◆ Write a clear explanation entitled 'Helping birds survive the winter'.

◆ Divide it into three paragraphs, each with a clear heading:

Paragraph 1: Explain clearly what the problems are for birds.

Paragraph 2: Suggest some things we can do to help.

Paragraph 3: Discuss the value of a bird table in the garden.

◆ Draw a labelled diagram.

Writing poetry

Read Unit 2.5 again, then choose one of these ideas to help you write a poem.

Days of the week

Make up a different verse for every day of the week, like this:

> *On Mondays in the mornings*
> *I hear a noisy din.*
> *The dustmen are a-coming*
> *To empty all the bins.*
> *BIFF! BANG! CRASH!*

Just up my street

A car has stopped at number four.
Two men are hammering on the door.
When I look out the window
And really stand and peer,
It is most extraordinary
What I can see and hear!

Think of an imaginary street. Write what you might see or hear going on.

Out of my window

A poem does not have to rhyme.
It could be just a list of things you see.

> *Bare, grey wintry trees,*
> *A watery sun in a washed-out sky,*
> *Robins scratching around for food.*

Handy hints on writing a poem

What type of poem?
◆ Will it rhyme?
◆ Will it have a chorus?
◆ Will it be divided into verses?

Make notes of your ideas.
◆ Choose the best ones.
◆ Cross out the others.

Read your notes again.
◆ Do you want to move any to a different place?
◆ Can you improve any or use better words?
◆ Ask someone else for their opinions.

◆ Check your spellings.
◆ Think how to set it out.
◆ Write a best copy.
◆ Illustrate your poem.

How are you getting on with the things in the chart? If you need extra practice, try the activities shown.

Grammar and punctuation	Apostrophes	1
	Adverbs with adjectives	2
	Commas	3
Spelling, phonics and vocabulary	Older and modern words	4
	Gender	5
	Over-used words	6
	Prefixes	7
	Spelling strategies	8, 9 and 1

1 Use apostrophes. Write the shortened form of each of the following. Do it like this: The pencil belonging to the boy – the boy's pencil

a) the ruler belonging to the teacher
b) the trunk of the elephant
c) the books belonging to the girls
d) the wings of the birds
e) the shoes belonging to the men
f) the hair of the children

2 Copy these sentences. Choose one of the adverbs below to go in front of each adjective.

very   quite   more   most

a) Ben was _____ intelligent than Edward.
b) The train was _____ near.
c) The naughty child was _____ silly.
d) Alice is the _____ studious child.

3 Copy the sentences. Put in the missing commas.

a) The dog was noisy barking at every visitor.
b) My new coat like the one in the window is very expensive.
c) By being careful Mr Patel was able to save enough for a holiday.
d) The car which was stolen was left outside the supermarket.

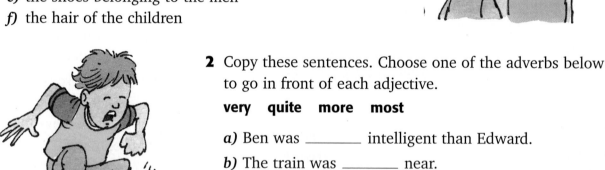

4 *a)* Divide these words into two sets – older and more modern words.

> **video   lantern   parlour   television   car   mangle   quill   computer   astronaut   stagecoach**

b) Now use a dictionary. Write the shortest definition you can for each one.

5 Write the masculine and feminine words that go together in pairs

> **husband   king   monk   stallion   drake   buck   queen   nun   wife   doe   mare   duck**

6 Copy the sentences. Replace each word 'nice' with a more interesting word each time.

> It was a nice day so Amir put on some nice clothes and went out. He passed lots of nice houses. Amir stopped and went into a nice shop to get a nice lolly.

7 Write six words that begin with the prefix 'al'. Check your spellings with a dictionary.

8 Copy these sentences and correct the spelling mistakes.

> It was a verey noisey scool. Poopils were frowing fings and showting. Suddenley the door floo open. In walkt the hed teecher. She was angrey. The chidren quickley went bak to there seets and got on quitely wiv they're wurk.

9 Think of one word containing each letter string.

> *a)* age   *b)* ail   *c)* air   *d)* ary   *e)* dge   *f)* augh
> *g)* ence   *h)* for   *i)* gue   *j)* ince   *k)* irm   *l)* ness
> *m)* oil   *n)* our   *o)* per   *p)* thr   *q)* ure

10 Write the root word contained in each of these words.

> *a)* thanked   *b)* quickly   *c)* effective   *d)* courageous
> *e)* foolish   *f)* metallic   *g)* starry   *h)* national
> *i)* laughter   *j)* acceptance

Handy hints for spelling

Look – Look carefully at the word.

Say – Say the word to hear how it sounds.

Cover – Cover the word and try to see it in your mind.

Write – Write the word from memory.

Check – Check your spelling with the original. Compare them.

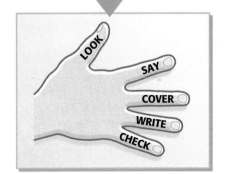

LOOK · SAY · COVER · WRITE · CHECK

The Journey

Granny's eyesight was getting worse. She needed to get a new pair of glasses but that involved a long, and sometimes hazardous, journey.

1 They ate their lunch on the roadside, in the shade of a whispering pine. There were chapatties and mango pickle and curry made from yams. They drank from a spring a little further down the path.

2 By late afternoon they were directly above Nain.

"We're almost there," said Mani. "I can see the temple near Raju-uncle's house."

"I can't see a thing," said Granny.

"That's because of the mist. There's a thick mist coming up the valley."

3 It began raining heavily as they entered the small market town on the banks of the river. Granny's umbrella was leaking badly. But they were soon drying themselves in Raju-uncle's house, and drinking glasses of sweet milky tea.

4 Mani got up early next morning and ran down the narrow street to bathe in the river. The swift but shallow mountain river was a tributary of the sacred Ganges, and its waters were held sacred too. As the sun rose, people thronged the steps leading down to the river, to bathe or pray or float flower-offerings downstream.

5 As Mani dressed, he heard the blare of a bus horn. There was only one bus to Mussoorie. He scampered up the slope, wondering if they'd miss it. But Granny was waiting for him at the bus stop. She had already bought their tickets.

6 The motor-road followed the course of the river, which thundered a hundred feet below. The bus was old and rickety, and rattled so much that the passengers could barely hear themselves speaking. One of them was pointing to a spot below, where another bus had gone off the road a few weeks back.

From Getting Granny's Glasses by Ruskin Bond

1 *a)* Who are the two main characters in the passage? *b)* Where are they headed for? *c)* Why are they going there?

2 List some of the clues that tell you the story took place in a different country. Include information about: *a)* the things Mani ate *b)* the things Mani saw *c)* the things Mani did *d)* the way Mani and his Granny were dressed.

3 *a)* What was the name of the sacred river that the mountain river ran into? *b)* How can you tell it was sacred? *c)* Which country was it in?

4 What sort of a person do you picture Granny to be? Why?

5 What do you think some of the difficulties and dangers were that Granny and Mani faced on their journey? Look in the passage for some clues.

6 Explain what each paragraph is all about, like this: Paragraph 1 is about Mani and Granny having a picnic.

NTENCE

1 Copy each of the following and say what class of word the underlined is, e.g. a noun, adjective or verb.
a) a <u>whispering</u> pine *b)* I bathed in a <u>spring</u>. *c)* The lion will <u>spring</u>.

2 Change each of these nouns into the plural, like this: lunch – lunches.
path temple curry lady glass bus church dish leaf thief

3 Copy each of these verbs, and then write it without its suffix.
raining entered drinking floated dressed wondering carrying married

4 Change the nouns in brackets to adjectives by adding a suffix, like this: a <u>misty</u> day (mist).
a) a _____ shirt (dirt) *b)* an _____ man (anger)
c) a _____ coin (gold) *d)* a _____ day (beauty)

R D

1 These compound words have got the wrong endings. Write each word correctly.
a) roadboard and cupside *b)* handstream and downbag
c) themcoat and waistselves *d)* keybone and backhole

2 Choose five of the compound words and write sentences with them in.

3 Mix the beginnings and endings of these words and make some silly compound words.
postcard toothbrush tablecloth headlines bookshelf crossroads shoelace

Leila

Leila was ten years old. She was a child of the desert, where the Bedouin travel on their camels through the endless expanse of shifting dunes. Leila ran like the wind. Her temper flashed like the swift streams that flooded the dry river beds after a storm. Among her people she was known as Leila the Wilful.

Leila's father, Sheik Tariq, was a just man, respected in all the desert encampments. But even Tariq could not tame his headstrong daughter Leila.

Leila had six brothers. The oldest was Hamed. He was Sheik Tariq's favourite son. Only he knew how to calm Leila when she was in a rage. Only he could make her laugh when she was gloomy and sad. Leila and Hamed went everywhere together.

One morning, as the last stars were fading in the sky, Hamed left the encampment. He mounted Sheik Tariq's white stallion and set off across the desert to seek out new pastures for the animals. From the top of the highest dune, Leila and her father waved as Hamed rode away.

Day after day went by, but Hamed did not return. Sheik Tariq set out to look for him, travelling from one oasis to the next, asking questions. Leila went with him.

A group of shepherds told them that they had seen a white stallion, far away on the horizon. But he carried no rider.

Passing merchants, their camels laden with spices for the bazaar, talked of the emptiness of the desert they had just travelled through. They said to Tariq, "Only Allah knows where your son is." Then Sheik Tariq knew that the sands had taken his son, like so many Bedouin before him.

When her father told Leila that she would never see Hamed again, she screamed and fell, beating the sand with her fist. No one could take her brother away from her, not even Allah! After a long time Tariq managed to calm her, and they started their long journey back to their encampment. As they travelled, Tariq fell silent. When they reached home he went to his tent and refused to eat anything, or to speak. Leila wandered blindly through the oasis, weeping.

After seven days, Tariq came out of his tent. He called his people together and said: "From this day forward, anyone who speaks Hamed's name will be severely punished. I wish to forget what I have lost." Sheik Tariq's expression was hard and cold. The Bedouin bowed their heads. They were all uneasy, but no one dared to utter a word.

From Leila by Sue Alexander and George Lemoine

T

1 *a)* What was the girl's name? *b)* Who was her father? *c)* Who was her oldest brother?

2 *a)* Describe the sort of girl Leila was. *b)* What sort of man was Tariq?
   c) Describe the sort of relationship she had with Hamed.

3 List some of the things you have discovered about the Bedouin.

4 *a)* Why did Hamed leave the encampment?
   b) What sort of things might have happened to Hamed in the desert?

5 What does "Only Allah knows where your son is." mean?

6 Describe the very different ways Tariq and Leila responded when they learnt about
   Hamed's disappearance. Say why you think each behaved as they did.

ATENCE

1 Fill in the missing form of the adjectives when you compare them.
   Do it like this: tall, taller, tallest.
   a) _____ , hotter, hottest   *b)* sad, _____ , saddest
   c) high, higher, _____   *d)* dry, _____ , driest

2 Add the suffix 'ly' to the adjectives to make them into adverbs.
   Do it like this: Tariq sat down heavily (heavy).
   a) Leila ran _____ (swift).   *b)* Hamed spoke _____ (calm).
   c) Leila waved _____ (happy).   *d)* The camels drank _____ (noisy).

3 Take the suffix off each adverb and write the adjective you are left with.
   Do it like this: wearily – weary.
   gratefully lazily cheaply steadily humbly poorly loyally sensibly

4 Copy and complete this: Many adverbs end with the suffix _____ .

RD

1 Write these diminutives in sets according to their endings:
   maiden sapling booklet kitten rosette seedling leaflet gosling

2 Write a definition for each diminutive. Use a dictionary to help you.

3 Think of all the characters you can whose names begin with Little.

4 Copy these sentences. Choose the correct word to complete them.
   a) The dog wagged (it's, its) tail.   *b)* Did you know (it's, its) raining?
   c) Look! (It's, Its) alive!   *d)* The car had lost (it's, its) wheels.

Annie's Story

When Annie's dad arrived he gave her a big hug. Annie tried not to hug him back.

"What shall we do this weekend, Annie?" asked Annie's dad. "It's your turn to choose."

"Nothing," said Annie.

The next day Annie and Matthew drove into the countryside with their dad. When they had parked, Matthew and Annie ran round to the back of the car. They watched their dad take out two huge kites. Matthew's was red with a dragon and Annie's was blue and yellow with a long tail. Matthew was excited.

"Thanks, Dad!" he shouted. "Can we fly them now?"

"Yes," said their dad. "The wind's just right. I'll show you how to get them going."

Annie followed behind, dragging her kite along the ground.

Soon Matthew had learned how to let the wind lift his kite high into the sky.

"Shall we get yours going, Annie?" asked her dad.

"No thanks," said Annie.

"Well, don't drag it like that – it might rip," he warned.

"Good," said Annie quietly.

At the top of the hill Annie sat down. She could see Matthew in the distance, flying his red kite.

"Don't you like your present?" asked Annie's dad. He sat down next to her. Annie was feeling cross and sad at the same time, but mostly she felt like crying.

"You're cross with me, aren't you?" asked her dad. Annie's dad went on talking. "I know I've hurt you by leaving home, Annie. I'm so sorry. I miss being with you and Matthew every day."

"You'll never come back to live, will you?" asked Annie.

"No," said her dad. "But we'll see each other every week. I'll make sure of that."

"Being hurt feels awful," said Annie.

"I know," said her dad. "Your Mum and I hurt each other – and now we're hurting you."

"It feels better when you talk about it, though," said Annie.

When Annie got into bed that night she gave her dad a big kiss. "I forgot to thank you for my kite," she said.

"You liked it really, then?" asked Annie's dad.

"Kites are lovely," said Annie, "but talking is better."

From Hurt *by Janine Amos*

T

1 *a)* What were the names of the two children? *b)* Who came to see them?
   c) Where did they go? *d)* What presents did the children receive?
2 *a)* Does Dad live at home? Give your reasons.
   b) How often do the children see their dad?
3 What do you think caused the marriage break-up?
4 Who seems most upset by the situation – Matthew or Annie? Say how you know.
5 How did Annie react *a)* when Dad first arrived *b)* when Dad gave her a kite
   c) when Dad sat down next to her with her kite?
6 Why do you think Annie said, 'Kites are lovely but talking is better.'?
7 How do you think Dad feels about the situation? Give your reasons.

NTENCE

1 Copy the sentences. Change the noun into an adjective to complete each one.
   Do it like this: Dad paid one of his weekly visits. (week)
   a) It was a _____ day. (wind) *b)* Dad gave Annie an _____ hug. (affection)
   c) The chair was _____ . (comfort)
2 Write the nouns from which these adjectives come, like this: dangerous – danger.
   a) terrible   *b)* sunny   *c)* mysterious   *d)* athletic   *e)* fortunate   *f)* accidental
3 Now make up sentences using the nouns you have made.

R D

1 Copy these words. Choose either 'w' or 'qu' to complete each word.
   a) _ ant *b)* _ addle   *c)* _ _ arrel   *d)* _ _ antity *e)* _ allet   *f)* _ _ alify
2 Write what you notice about the sound of the letter 'a' in these words.
3 Copy these words. Complete each word with 'or'.
   a) w _ _ m   *b)* w _ _ d   *c)* w _ _ ld   *d)* w _ _ th
4 Write sentences containing each of the words in question 3.
5 Complete these words with the letter 'a'.
   a) f _ ther   *b)* m _ st   *c)* _ fter   *d)* b _ sket   *e)* cl _ sp   *f)* gr _ ss
6 Complete these words with 'al'.
   a) c _ _ m   *b)* c _ _ f   *c)* p _ _ m   *d)* h _ _ f   *e)* ps _ _ m   *f)* qu _ _ m
7 Write what you notice about the sound of 'a' and 'al' in the words in questions
   5 and 6.

All Fools' Day

First voice

Look you bicycle wheel
turning round!
*When you look down
you feel like a clown.*

Chorus

Yay, Yay,
Today is All Fools' Day!

Second voice

Look you drop a penny
pon the ground!
*When you think you lucky
and look down,
Not a thing like money
pon the ground.*

Chorus

Yay, Yay,
Today is All Fools' Day!

Third voice

Look you shoelace loose out!
*When you hear the shout
and look down at you shoe
It ain't true, it ain't true.*

Chorus

Yay, Yay,
Today is All Fools' Day!

Fourth voice

Look you mother calling you!
Look you mother calling you!
Is true, is true, is true!

First voice

*Well let she call till she is blue,
I ain't going nowhay.
You ain't ketching me this time
Today is All Fools' Day.*

Mother's voice

Kenrick! Kenrick! Kenrrriicckk!
See how long I calling this boy
and he playing he ain't hear.
When he come I gon cut he tail!

John Agard

T

1 What joke is being played on the boy in each verse?

2 *a)* What is the boy's name? How do you know? *b)* How does he feel?

3 *a)* What does the fourth voice call out? *b)* Does Kenrick believe it? *c)* Is it true?

4 *a)* Why does his mother say his name like this – "Kenrrriicckk"?
What does this tell you? *b)* How can you tell his mother is cross?

5 *a)* Find and copy a rhyming couplet in the poem. *b)* Write down the chorus.

6 What clues are there in the poem that it is not set in Britain?

7 The poet writes in a slightly different form of English. *a)* Find three examples of this in the poem. *b)* Write them down how you would say them.

8 Make up your own April Fool's Day poem with a chorus.

TENCE

1 Say which of the following is a statement, a question, an exclamation and an order.
a) May I stay out a little longer?   *b)* Go home at once.
c) When you look down you feel like a clown.   *d)* Look out – your mum's coming!

2 Change these statements into questions.
a) My shoelace is undone.   *b)* You did your homework last night.
c) They were on their way home.   *d)* She is going to the shops.

3 Turn the questions into orders, like this: Have you fed the dog? Feed the dog.
a) Have you watered the plants?   *b)* May I have some crisps?
c) Can you come out to play?   *d)* Have you mended the puncture?

D

1 The 'a' in 'mad' is a short vowel. The 'a' in 'made' is a long vowel.
a) Think of five short words that end in 'k', like 'back'.
b) Think of five short words that end in 'ke', like 'bake'.
c) What do you notice about the sound of the middle vowel in each set of words?

2 *a)* Write five words starting with 'kn'. *b)* What do you notice about them?

3 *a)* Write down five words beginning with 'v'. *b)* Is 'v' always followed by a vowel or a consonant? *c)* Think of five words that have 'v' near the end, e.g. give. *d)* Is 'v' always followed by a vowel or a consonant? *e)* Can you find any word that ends with 'v'? *f)* Can you think of any word that has a consonant coming immediately in front of a 'v'?

Nnenna and Mrs Ezelu

1   Nnenna tried her best to raise her father's spirits. She cooked all his favourite meals. She cleaned his treasured ornaments. She even polished his hoe every night, just as she had seen her mother do. But her father still looked unhappy.

2   One day, Nnenna's father came back from the farm looking very excited. He had a great big smile on his face. Nnenna was glad to see him in such good spirits. She picked up the fresh corn and yams he had brought back with him. After washing them, she went into the backyard to start the fire.

3   That night, as they sat by the fire roasting the corn, Nnenna's father told her why he was looking so happy.

"I met a very nice woman today," he began. "I've invited her round on Sunday. Her name is Mrs Ezelu and she lives by the edge of the farm. I think she just moved there."

Nnenna didn't say anything. She was glad her father was looking his old self again. After the moon rose, Nnenna's father went into the house. He whistled as he took off his work clothes. For the first time in weeks he slept soundly.

4   Mrs Ezelu and her children arrived early on Sunday morning. Nnenna had dusted and cleaned the house. It was sparkling. The meal they had prepared was delicious – garri with banga soup. After eating, Mrs Ezelu insisted on washing up all the plates.

"Both of you have done enough for one day," she said. "Go and rest your feet. I'll look after everything."

Nnenna did not need any encouraging. She had been up early that day and cooking the meal had exhausted her. Nnenna took her mat into the yard and lay down for an afternoon nap.

5   The wedding ceremony followed soon after, and Mrs Ezelu and her children moved in. Nnenna was pleased because she could see that her father was happy. And she thought Mrs Ezelu was a nice enough woman.

6   Once Mrs Ezelu had settled in as Nnenna's stepmother, her attitude towards Nnenna changed. She never let Nnenna rest, shouting and screaming at her.

"Don't just sit there, you horrible girl," she would say when Nnenna got back from school. "Come on, go and wash the children's clothes. There's plenty of work to do around here, lazy girl."

From Isimeme Stories by Isimeme Ibazebo

1 *a)* What was the girl's name? *b)* How did she try to cheer her father up?
c) Why do you think her father was sad?

2 *a)* How can you tell Nnenna loved her father?
b) Why did he come home excited one day?

3 *a)* How did Mrs Ezelu behave when she visited Nnenna's house for the first time?
b) How did she change once she had married Nnenna's father?
c) What do you think of Mrs Ezelu? Give your reasons.

4 List some of the clues that tell you the story took place in a different country.
Notice *a)* the names *b)* the things they ate *c)* the things they did *d)* other clues.

5 Notice how the passage is divided into paragraphs. Each paragraph tells you
something different. Write a sentence about each paragraph. Explain what it is all
about. Do it like this: Paragraph 1 is about Nnenna trying to cheer her father up.

ʌ T E N C E

1 Copy the sentences and punctuate them correctly.
a) after washing the yams nnenna went outside
b) later that night as they sat by the fire nnennas father told her about mrs ezelu
c) he said I met a very nice woman today
d) nnenna replied Im very happy for you youre looking more like your old self

2 Write the words below in two sets:

SET A:	those you can add a suffix to, e.g. tell – telling.
SET B:	those you cannot add a suffix to, e.g. into.

tell into during wash sleep across against snap kick beyond

3 Label the sets as verbs or prepositions.

ʀ D

1 Think of ten short words (of five letters or less) that end in 'ss'.

2 Divide the words below into two sets according to where the 'ss' comes.
goodness missile pressure kindness crossing cleanliness smallness

3 Learn the words using the *Look, say, cover, write, check* method.

4 Divide the words below into two sets according to where the 'll' comes.
fall follow pillar bell allowed till valley roll full hillock

5 Label the sets as words of one syllable or two syllables.

Review your reading habits

1 Copy and complete this reading review. Choose the words which express your thoughts best.

- ◆ I think reading is (important/unimportant) because...
- ◆ I (enjoy/do not enjoy) reading because...
- ◆ I read (a lot/very little) because...
- ◆ I prefer (fiction/non-fiction/both) because...
- ◆ List some reasons why you think people read.
- ◆ List some of the types of stories you like best.
  Choose from stories that:
  - make you laugh or cry
  - are about history
  - make you think or imagine
  - are about animals
  - are about everyday life
  - are about real people and problems
  - are about other countries
  - are about space and the future
- ◆ Who is your favourite author?
- ◆ What is the best book you have ever read?

Developing a story

2 Use the characters and setting from a story you have read. Develop the plot in your own way. Here are some ideas.

It Happened to my Gran

Read Unit 3.1 again. Imagine you are Mani. Think of something terrible that could happen. Perhaps:

- ◆ the bus crashes and your Gran is badly injured.
- ◆ you are in the mountains and Gran falls ill. You have to leave her and seek help.
- ◆ something else happens?

Write about the situation; what you feel and think; what you do.

The Desert Experience

Read Unit 3.2 again. Imagine you are Leila.

Choose your own way to finish the story. Perhaps:

Hamed never returns. How do you cope with his death?

you go to search for him. Is he alive? injured?

Hamed eventually returns. What happened to him?

The Trouble with Step-Mothers

Read Unit 3.5 again. Imagine you are Nnenna.

The situation at home gets worse. Do you:

run away? Why? What about your father? What happens?

confront the situation and tell your father? What do you say? How do you feel?

How does he take it? What does he do?

do something else?

Writing a short story about a moral dilemma

- ◆ You are shopping in town.
- ◆ Suddenly, 'Buster' Braggins comes up behind you.
- ◆ You are scared of him.
- ◆ He threatens to hurt you unless you help him steal a CD.
- ◆ He forces you to put one in your bag.
- ◆ As you leave the shop you drop your bag. The CD falls out.
- ◆ An assistant comes to help and sees it.
- ◆ You look round. Buster has disappeared. What do you do?
- ◆ Write the story.

Writing a longer story

- ◆ Read Unit 3.3 again. Imagine you are in a similar situation.
- ◆ You live at home, but your parents do not get on.
- ◆ You fear there will be a break-up.
- ◆ Write a story.
- ◆ Try to express your thoughts, feelings and concerns.
- ◆ Choose whichever ending you wish.

Handy hints for planning stories

Setting

Where will your story take place?

Will it take place in the past, now or in the future?

Characters

Who will be in your story: people you know, made-up people or animals?

What will they look like? What sort of things will they do and say?

Plot

What will your story be about?

How will it begin? What sort of things will happen in the middle?

How will the story end – will it be sad, happy, exciting or mysterious?

> How are you getting on with the things in the chart? If you need extra practice, try the activities shown.

Grammar and punctuation	Classes of words	1 and 2
	Types of sentences	3 and 4
	Verbs and prepositions	5
Spelling, phonics and vocabulary	Compound words	6
	Diminutives	7
	Spelling strategies	8, 9 and 1

1 Copy these and say whether the underlined word is a noun (N), adjective (Adj), verb (V) or adverb (Adv).
Do it like this: two <u>houses</u> (N)

a) I <u>bake</u> cakes.   *b)* Come <u>quickly</u>.
c) a green <u>dragon</u>   *d)* the spotted <u>dog</u>
e) I sing <u>loudly</u>.   *f)* <u>cold</u> feet
g) A door <u>banged</u>.   *h)* <u>glass</u> windows

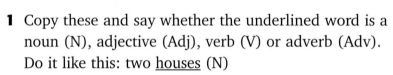

2 *a)* Write the plural of these nouns:

key   loaf   box   fairy   potato

b) Write the verb that each noun comes from, like this:
collection – collect

marriage   advertisement   resistance   pressure

c) Make an adjective from each noun, like this:
danger – dangerous

favour   marvel   beauty   child   comfort   friend

d) Make an adverb from each adjective, like this:
proud – proudly

clever   sudden   lucky   heavy   sensible   grateful

3 Copy each sentence. Say if it is a statement (S), question (Q), exclamation (E) or an order (O).

a) Give it to me.   *b)* Can you give it to me?
c) Quick! Give it to me now!   *d)* I gave it to him.

4 Change these statements into questions:

a) This is the way to London.   *b)* He makes cakes.
c) She runs fast.

5 Copy the sentences. Underline the verb in each. Cross out the preposition.

a) The cat sat on the mat.   *b)* The train raced through the tunnel.   *c)* A squirrel climbed up a tree.   *d)* Mum went into the shop.

6 Write the compound words as sums, like this:
black + berry = blackberry

a) tablecloth   *b)* postcard   *c)* handbag   *d)* cupboard
e) snowfall   *f)* firelight   *g)* snowman   *h)* butterfly

7 Write the diminutive form of each, like this: lion – cub

a) cat   *b)* dog   *c)* goat   *d)* duck   *e)* hen   *f)* pig

8 Copy and complete each word with a suitable letter or letters.

a) w _ rld   *b)* w _ ter   *c)* qu _ rrel   *d)* w _ r
e) b _ sket   *f)* p _ _ m   *g)* ra _ e   *h)* _ erse
i) ha _ ves

9 Make up sentences including all the words you have made.

10 *a)* Find and write all the words with two syllables from the High Frequency Word List (Term 3) on page 96.
b) Use the *Look, say, cover, write, check* method to help you learn them.
c) Make up some sentences and use the words in them.

Handy hints for spelling

1 Is the word spelt as it sounds? Does it contain any phonemes you already know?

2 Does the word look right? Do you know any other words like it?

3 Can you break the word into smaller parts? Which is the most difficult part of the word?

4 Do you know what the word means?

5 Have you used a word book or dictionary to help you?

LOOK
SAY
COVER
WRITE
CHECK

Our Feathered Friends

In the local newspaper there have recently been several letters on the subject of caged birds.

Dear Editor

It is wicked to exploit birds for profit and expose them to needless suffering. Harmless birds are trapped and transported in terrible conditions. Over 50% of birds transported from abroad do not survive the journey. Birds cannot protect themselves from humans. They should have the freedom to choose where they live. How would the manager of BirdLand like to be caged up all his life?

Yours despairingly

Ali Rafizadeh

Dear Editor

What's all the fuss about? I'm 82 and have had a budgie for years. She never complains! She is such good company for me.

Yours caringly
Mrs Edna Cook

Dear Editor

I am a member of SBFO (Set Birds Free Organisation). We believe it is cruel and unnatural to cage birds. Cages, where birds have little room to fly, are poor substitutes for the forests and woodlands from which they come. In cages they cannot search or hunt for their own food. Birds cannot speak so we speak for them: Set them free!

Yours disgustedly

Tania Smith

Dear Editor

I feel I must reply to some of the misguided letters about BirdLand. All the birds in the zoo are well treated. They are provided with fresh food and water each day and their cages are cleaned regularly. We have a zoo vet on site to ensure the birds are in good health. Indeed, it has been proved that 95% of the birds survive longer in BirdLand than in the wild. The cages are spacious, with ample room for the birds to stretch their wings. We try to keep the caged environment as natural as possible. At BirdLand we pride ourselves on saving many species from extinction. In their natural habitats they are fighting for survival against deforestation and use of chemicals in farming.

Yours faithfully

Brian Mayberry
(Manager of BirdLand)

Dear Editor

My family had a great day at BirdLand. The children loved it. As well as being an education, it also brings money and business into our town.

Yours

Mrs Newton

FREE THE BIRDS!

CLOSE BIRDLAND

1 *a)* What are all the letters about?

b) Which people support caging birds? *c)* Which people are against it?

2 List as many points as you can find for and against caging birds.

3 Mr Rafizadeh is trying to persuade people to think as he does. Copy his letter and underline some of the powerful words he uses. Do it like this: It is <u>wicked</u> to <u>exploit</u> birds for profit and <u>expose</u> them to <u>needless suffering</u>.

4 Now copy Brian Mayberry's letter. Underline the strong words he uses, like this:

I feel I <u>must</u> reply to some of the <u>misguided</u> letters about BirdLand. All the birds in the zoo are <u>well treated</u>.

5 Which of the two letters above uses a lot of *a)* positive words *b)* negative words?

6 Both Mr Rafizadeh and Brian Mayberry give a statistic in their letters to support their argument. Find these and write them down.

ENCE

1 Use information in the letters to give your views about caged birds.

2 Write three paragraphs. In the first paragraph give one side of the argument.

3 In the second paragraph give the opposing viewpoint.

4 In the third paragraph explain that you have considered both sides of the argument. End up by stating strongly your own viewpoint.

RD

1 See how many 'tion' words you can find in the letters opposite.

2 Make these verbs into nouns, like this: protect – protection.

inspect   subtract   obstruct   direct   attract

3 Make up sentences containing each of the 'tion' words you have made.

4 Make these verbs into nouns, like this: educate – education.

decorate   generate   create   congratulate   communicate

5 Make nouns from these verbs, like this: organise – organisation.

prepare   explore   imagine   reserve   examine

6 Sort these words into two groups according to their endings:

television   permission   decision   admission   expression   explosion

John and the Green Dragon

It was the night of the Chinese New Year.
The swing doors flapped to and fro as steaming
dishes were carried through to hungry people.
The smells wafted upstairs, but John did not stir.

Outside, the moon hung like a great lantern. Suddenly a shadow darkened the moonlit sky. John awoke. He could hear a rustling and a whirling – like wind; a crackling and sparkling – like waves. Outside his window John saw a green head bobbing up and down – a dragon's head – with red, glowing eyes and a long, flaming tongue darting in and out between huge, spiky, white teeth. The dragon squeezed himself between the open windows. His jagged, green body and long, long tail came trailing inside and coiled itself around the room like a giant kite.

"Hello," said John politely. "Can I help you?"

"I've flown all the way from China," said the Green Dragon. "Over snowy mountains and icy lakes; winding rivers and smoking factories; over vast fields of rice and wheat – and now I'm so hungry I could swallow up your mother's kitchen."

"Oh, please don't do that," cried John. "My mother and father are very proud of their kitchen. They say we cook the best Chinese food outside London. I help too with sorting out the knives, forks and spoons, and our customers call me Hong Kong John."

"Well then, Hong Kong John," said the dragon, "since I'm so hungry, and since it is Chinese New Year, I think I should savour some of your famous food. After all – I am an expert. I have eaten at the finest tables in China – at feasts given by the great emperors themselves!"

"You must be very old if you have eaten with emperors of China," said John.

"Several hundred – maybe even a thousand," boasted the dragon. "Now then – I would like to eat deep fried pork with delectable seaweed; braised beef with soya sauce and noodles; bean curd with crab meat; king fried prawns with heavenly vegetables of the four seasons; but to start with I must sharpen my teeth on succulent spare ribs, and I'll finish with a bowl of lychees to sweeten me up. All this must be accompanied with a constant flow of hot, sweet-scented Jasmine tea – pots and pots of it. Well? What are you waiting for?" The Green Dragon looked at John impatiently.

"I ... I can't get all that!" gasped John.

"Can't you?" The dragon whisked his tail and ground his teeth.

Jamila Gavin

T

1 Copy and complete these sentences about the story with suitable words:

The boy's name was _____ . His parents cooked _____ _____ .
It was the night of the _____ _____ _____ .
A _____ _____ came to visit John. It had come from _____ .

2 What sounds did John hear that woke him up?

3 Describe how the dragon looked.

4 List the things the dragon had passed on his journey.

5 What problem was John faced with at the end of the passage?

6 How can you tell the dragon was getting impatient?

7 Think of a different way to end the story.

8 Who wrote the story? (Try and find some more books to read by the same author.)

NTENCE

1 A dash is a small line (–) and is sometimes used to separate ideas instead of a comma, like this: He could hear a rustling and a whirling – like wind. Find three other examples of a dash being used on the page opposite.

2 Copy each sentence and put in the missing dash.

a) The children had three pets a dog and two cats.
b) There is only one place worth visiting in Paris the Eiffel Tower.

3 A hyphen looks like a dash. It is often used to join two words together. Copy the sentences and complete each with one of the double words below:

double-edged   light-fingered   gold-plated

a) The thief was rather _____ . *b)* Emma was wearing a _____ ring.
c) The soldier had a _____ sword.

RD

1 Add the suffix 'able' to the nouns to make them into adjectives.
enjoy   wash   reason   remark   fashion

2 Change these nouns into adjectives, like this: love – lovable
admire   excuse   value   desire   compare

3 Make up a rule for what happened to the words in question 2.

4 Use a dictionary to decide if these words should end in 'ible' or 'able'.

a) horr _____   *b)* respons _____   *c)* consider _____

79

The Hidden Persuaders

1

Desirable Dogs Demand...

DOGGIE DROPS

2

ACT NOW!

HELP FEED THOSE IN NEED

Act Now...

| **Please send cheques to:** |
| Needing Food, 34-56 Parklake Row, |
| Gonemere, Lakelands, |
| Fostershire FR3 4RT. |

3

25% Off all prices

SALE

Last Few Days

Everything must go

4

LADIES MOUNTAIN BIKE

10 speed; alloy brakes and handlebars; black and silver. Must be seen.
Tel: 011234 888888

5

CHOCO CRUNCH

Best of the Bunch... that's CHOCO CRUNCH

The NEW taste sensation

Thick creamy chocolate coating
Nutty crunchy filling

BE THE FIRST TO TRY ONE
YOU'LL **NEVER** BE THE SAME

Check your wrappers –
Super video games to be won

6

WEBBS ESTATE AGENT

Alfred Street, Northlands

A well-maintained semi-detached house in a leafy suburb; set in quiet residential street; close to schools, park and shops. Easy access to town centre by bus or car route.

- Bedrooms – 3 good-size rooms, wardrobes
- Reception – living room and dining area
- Kitchen – modern and well equipped
- Bathroom – shower and bath (ivory)
- Garage – spacious
- Garden – neat and well-kept

PRICE £85,000

T

1 Which advertisement is *a)* asking for money *b)* advertising a sale *c)* advertising a house *d)* selling a bicycle *e)* telling people about a new sweet?

2 *a)* Which advertisement uses alliteration? *b)* Which two advertisements include a rhyme? *c)* Which two advertisements consist mainly of facts?

3 How is advertisement 3 trying to persuade people to come into the shop?

4 Sometimes adverts do not tell you everything. Think of four things the estate agents might not have told you about the house in advertisement 6.

5 *a)* What claims have the advertisers made in no. 5? *b)* Why have they used a teenager in the advert? *c)* List the persuasive words like 'new' that have been used. *d)* Why are some words in capital letters? *e)* What does the advert tell you about the ingredients of the chocolate bar?

6 Which advertisement *a)* appeals to you most? Why? *b)* is most honest? *c)* has the best design? Why?

NTENCE

1 Find a colon (:) in an advertisement opposite. Copy the part of the advertisement containing it and explain how it is being used.

2 Two advertisements contain two semi-colons (;). Copy these parts of the advertisements and explain how the semi-colons are being used.

3 Copy and punctuate the following sentences:

a) I want you to buy some things for me string scissors tape labels and paper
b) mr patel shouted to the driver dont forget to get me to the station by two oclock
c) there in the corner of the room stood a beautifully laid table
d) Im ready to see you please come and explain whats happened the teacher said

RD

1 *a)* Copy these words: tough, through, trough, plough. *b)* Underline the common letter string in each. *c)* Say what you notice about the way the words are pronounced. *d)* Write sentences using the words.

2 *a)* Copy these words: hour, journey, could, route, four. *b)* Underline the common letter string in each. *c)* Say what you notice about the way the words are pronounced. *d)* Write sentences using the words.

3 Copy the sets of words below. Underline the odd one out in each set.

a) moth, brother, cloth, frothy   *b)* kind, find, spindle, mind
c) wounded, bounded, sounded, rounded   *d)* mice, police, twice, splice

A Pot-Pourri of Poems

1

Geraldine Giraffe
(a long, thin poem!)

The
longest
ever
woolly
scarf
was
worn by
Geraldine
Giraffe.
Around
her
neck
the
scarf
she
wound
but
still
it
trailed
upon
the
ground
Colin West

2

A list poem

Happiness is a pair of new trainers
Happiness is finishing a jigsaw,
Happiness is a warm puppy,
Happiness is a wobbly tooth,
Happiness is ....

3

An alphabet poem

A is for Albert
Who breaks all his toys

B is for Betty
Who runs after boys

C is for Clara
With the red, sniffy nose

D is for Derek
Who's got smelly toes

E is for Edward
He never washes his face

F is for Fred
Who looks a disgrace!

4

Haiku *(17 syllables)*

A tail-swishing cat (5)
Lies waiting in the bushes (7)
Birds peck unaware (5)

5

Cinquain *(22 syllables)*

I saw (2)
Six silly snails (4)
Sliding on dustbin lids (6)
They slipped and slithered and fell off. (8)
Crick! Crack! (2)

T

1 Which poem is about *a)* snails *b)* happiness *c)* children *d)* a cat *e)* a giraffe?

2 Which are *a)* rhyming poems *b)* non-rhyming poems?

3 Which of the first two poems has a strong rhythm?

4 Why do you think poem 1 is set out as it is? (Look in some poetry books and try and find some more poems by Colin West.)

5 Why is poem 2 called a 'list poem'?

6 Which poems consist of a set number of syllables? (Say each type of poem aloud, tap out the syllables and check the number in each line.)

7 How many stanzas are there in poem 3?

8 Which poem *a)* was your favourite? Why? *b)* did you like least? Why?

TENCE

1 Copy the sentences. Think of a suitable conjunction for each gap.
a) Around her neck the scarf she wound _____ still it trailed upon the ground.
b) Shahla did not know _____ to choose the red or pink dress.
c) They sat on the beach _____ the sun set.

2 Use 'who', 'whose' or 'which' to complete each sentence.
a) Albert is a boy _____ breaks all his toys.
b) I met an Italian girl _____ name was Gina.
c) Our teacher told us about the camel, _____ can be called the 'ship of the desert'.

3 Make up some sentences of your own, using these conjunctions:
although   because   until   but   unless

RD

1 Copy the sets of words. Underline the common root in each. (The first set is done for you.) Write a definition for each word. Use a dictionary to help.
a) im<u>part</u>, a<u>part</u>, de<u>part</u>ure   *b)* invent, prevent, advent
c) pressure, depress, impress   *d)* telephone, microphone, gramophone

2 Think of a longer word containing each of these words. Do it like this: wool – woolly.
a) long   *b)* round   *c)* trail   *d)* train   *e)* sniff   *f)* wash   *g)* grace   *h)* dust

3 Think of a word with the same letter string as the one underlined.
a) w<u>oo</u>l   *b)* s<u>car</u>   *c)* tr<u>ail</u>   *d)* <u>night</u>   *e)* br<u>eak</u>   *f)* p<u>air</u>   *g)* t<u>oes</u>   *h)* b<u>ush</u>

Looking after the Earth

If the Earth were only a few feet in diameter, floating a few feet above a field somewhere, people would come from everywhere to marvel at it. People would walk around it, marvelling at its big pools of water, its little pools and the water flowing between the pools. People would marvel at the bumps on it, and the holes in it, and they would marvel at the very thin layer of gas surrounding it and the water suspended in the gas. The people would marvel at all the creatures walking around the ball, and at the creatures in the water. The people would declare it as sacred because it was the only one, and they would protect it so that it would not be hurt. The ball would be the greatest wonder known, and the people would come to pray to it, to be healed, to gain knowledge, to know beauty and to wonder how it could be. People would love it, and defend it with their lives because they would somehow know that their lives, their own roundness, could be nothing without it. If the Earth were only a few feet in diameter.

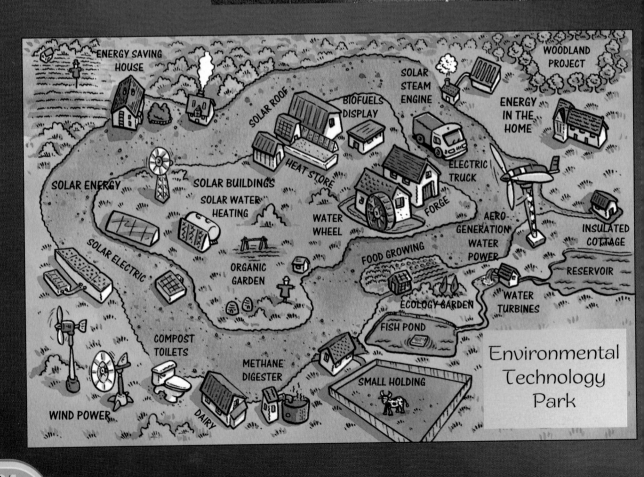

T

1 Copy and complete these sentences:

 a) 1 is a poster about the _____ . *b)* 2 is a plan of _____ .

2 What is the poster referring to when it says: *a)* its big pools of water *b)* the bumps on it *c)* the thin layer of gas surrounding it *d)* the water suspended in the gas?

3 *a)* In what ways does the poster say that people would behave differently towards the Earth if it were only a few feet in diameter? *b)* Why do you think this is?

4 *a)* What do you think of the poster? Give your opinion.

 b) How does the poster persuade you to think about conservation?

5 Look at the plan. Say whether you would find each of the following at the Park

 a) reservoir *b)* airport *c)* fish pond *d)* supermarket *e)* water wheel *f)* forge

6 If you visited the Park, which three things would you particularly want to see?

7 What sort of life-style is the Park trying to persuade people to think about?

8 In what way are the poster and the map similar?

TENCE

1 Change each of these positive statements into a negative form, like this:
 The Earth is round. The Earth is not round.

 a) There are big pools of water. *b)* The creatures walk on the ground.
 c) Rain comes from the clouds. *d)* People care about the Earth.

2 Change each negative statement into a positive one.

 a) The girl cannot hear the car coming. *b)* The party was not very good.
 c) Frozen water is not ice. *d)* The children did not come from Wales.

3 Change each statement into a question.

 a) People came from everywhere. *b)* The girl can swim.
 c) A circle has a diameter. *d)* The house is designed to save energy.

R D

1 Find words on the poster containing these letter strings:
 a) ear *b)* oat *c)* low *d)* pen *e)* eat *f)* won *g)* ledge *h)* end *i)* meter

2 Find words on the map ending with these suffixes:
 a) ive *b)* ic *c)* ar *d)* ing *e)* tion *f)* oir *g)* er *h)* ogy

3 Use a dictionary to find the meanings of the following words:

 solar   organic   ecology   generator   technology   conservation

Points of view

1 Copy a chart like this. Think of at least five good reasons to put in each column.

> All children should do at least an hour's homework each night!

Reasons for homework	Reasons against homework
It gives you a chance to practise what you learn in school.	School is for work – home is for leisure.

◆ Write two different letters to Mrs Cratchit, the politician. One should support her view. The other should state an opposing viewpoint.

Name of product, big and bold

Use of rhyming jingle and alliteration

Mouth-watering description

Makes people feel they have to have one

Uses teenager to appeal to children

Stresses that it is new

An extra bonus

Advertising

2 Look at the features on this advertisement and the other in Unit 3.8.

◆ Make up your own adver

◆ Persuade people to buy a new product called Cruncho Crisps.

◆ Do it in rough first so you can experiment, change things and cross things ou

◆ Make it colourful and eye-catching.

◆ Set it out with a clear, easy-to-read message.

◆ Use all the ideas you hav learned.

riting poetry

Use the poems in Unit 3.9 to help you write some poems of your own.

long, thin poem

Write about a factory chimney, a skyscraper or something else long and thin.

Set it out like the giraffe poem.

list poem

Choose a theme like 'Sadness', 'Holidays' or the name of a colour.

Write each idea on a separate line.

n alphabet poem

Make up an alphabet of food, of animals, or of things found in your bedroom.

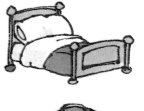

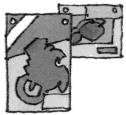

'count the syllables' poem

Write a Haiku, or Cinquain poem.

Focus on just one thing.

Consider it in detail and jot down your ideas.

Add or take away words to get the correct number of syllables.

Say the poem aloud and check the number of syllables!

Handy hints on drafting and editing

Jot your thoughts down in rough.

Choose your best ideas and work on them.

Move words around.
Add or take away words.

Use descriptive words.

Make a best copy.

Think about how you will set out your work.

Have you punctuated it correctly?

Have you checked for silly spelling mistakes?

Have you looked up any words you are not sure of?

Is your handwriting easy to read?

Are you going to use the computer?

How are you getting on with the things in the chart? If you need extra practice, try the activities shown.

Grammar and punctuation	Dashes	1
	Hyphens	2
	Colons and semi-colons	3
	Conjunctions	4
	Positive and negative sentences	5
	Punctuation (general)	6
Spelling, phonics and vocabulary	Common word endings	7 and 8
	Roots of words	9
	Spelling strategies	10

1 Copy each sentence. Put the missing dash in each.

a) There is only one way to please my teacher by trying hard.

b) I wish I had some money lots of money!

c) I love London a very busy city.

2 Make up some sentences. Include these words with hyphens in them.

upside-down   hard-working   freshly-baked

3 Copy the sentences. After each, write if it contains a colon or semi-colon.

a) For your trip you will need: a passport, your tickets and some money.

b) The guide opened the door; inside the room he showed us the king's throne.

4 Copy the sentences. Underline the conjunction in each.

a) You do not have to go unless you want to.

b) We are going on holiday because the weather is so lovely.

c) We looked everywhere for the book but could not find it.

5 Change these positive sentences into negative ones.

a) The weather is beautiful.   *b)* It rained hard.

c) We saw the procession.

d) Handel wrote some wonderful music.

6 Punctuate these sentences correctly.

a) heres the treasure I think it is the lost pirates gold he shouted excitedly

b) wheres the knife the chef asked looking all round the kitchen

c) its a long way to dover a very long way

7 Copy these words. Finish them with 'tion', 'sion' or 'ssion'. Use a dictionary to check if you are not sure.

a) decora ___   *b)* admi ___   *c)* divi ___   *d)* posi ___
e) televi ___   *f)* sec ___   *g)* confe ___   *h)* progre ___
i) pen ___   *j)* inven ___   *k)* permi ___   *l)* colli ___

8 Complete the words with 'able' or 'ible'. Use a dictionary to check your answers.

a) horr ___   *b)* cap ___   *c)* terr ___   *d)* prob ___
e) flex ___   *f)* remark ___

9 Copy the sets of words. Underline the common root in each. Write a definition for each word. Use a dictionary to help.

a) abuse   misuse   refuse
b) inquest   request   question
c) vision   revise   invisible
d) export   import   important
e) geography   photograph   autograph
f) television   telescope   telegraph

0 *a)* Copy ten tricky words from the High Frequency Word List (Term 3) on page 96.

b) Underline the tricky bit in each word.

c) Use the *Look, say, cover, write, check* method for learning the words.

d) Make up some sentences and include the words in them.

on page 96.

Handy hints for spelling

LOOK – Look carefully at the word.

SAY – Say the word to hear how it sounds.

COVER – Cover the word and try to see it in your mind.

WRITE – Write the word from memory.

CHECK – Check your spelling with the original. Compare them.

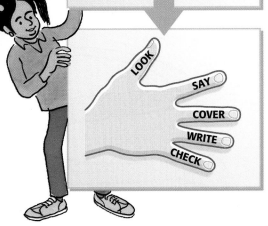

LOOK
SAY
COVER
WRITE
CHECK

Glossary

adjective

An adjective is a describing word. It describes (adds meaning to) a noun. For example:

a **fat** cat

When we compare nouns we use comparative adjectives. For example:

fat – **fatter**

adverb

An adverb is a word that gives more meaning to a verb. Adverbs often tell us how something happened. They often end in 'ly'. For example:

The dog barked **loudly**.

agreement

Agreement is a link between words to show that they go together. For example:

The cow moos

The cow, the subject of the sentence, agrees with **moos**, which is the verb.

alliteration

Alliteration is when we use lots of words that begin with the same sound. For example:

Snakes **s**lide **s**lowly.

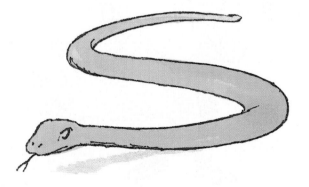

alphabetical order

Alphabetical order means words are put in order according to the letter or letters they begin with. These words are in alphabetical order:

ant, **b**ear, **c**at, **d**og

apostrophe

An apostrophe is like a raised comma. It is used in two ways:

1 In contractions (when words are shortened by leaving out letters). The apostrophe shows something has been missed out. For example:

do not can be written as **don't**

2 To show possession. For example:

the book belonging to the girl
= the **girl's** book

the book belonging to the girls
= the **girls'** book

author

An author is someone who writes books.

characters

Characters are the names of people, animals or things that appear in stories.

chorus

A chorus is a part of a poem or song that is usually repeated after each verse.

class of word

Words may be grouped in different classes according to the job they do. For example:

nouns   adjectives   verbs

colon

A colon is often used to introduce a list, or before someone speaks or instead of a full stop. For example:

He was very cold: the temperature was below zero.

comma

A comma is a punctuation mark. It tells you to pause. For example:

I went home, had a sandwich and watched TV.

comparative adjectives

(See adjective)

compound word

A compound word is made from two words which are joined to make one longer word. For example:

butter + fly = **butterfly**

conjunction

A conjunction is a joining word. Conjunctions may be used to join two sentences together. For example:

I put up my umbrella **when** it started to rain.

connective

Connectives are words used to link together different parts of a text. For example:

He said he was too tired to come out; **in other words** he didn't want to play.

(Conjunctions are also connectives.)

consonant

Letters can be divided into vowels and consonants. The vowels are **a, e, i, o** and **u.** The rest of the letters of the alphabet are consonants.

contents page

A contents page appears at the beginning of a book. It tells you the names of the sections or chapters in the book.

contraction

(See apostrophe)

dash

A dash holds words apart. It is stronger than a comma, but not as strong as a full stop. For example:

There is only one meal worth eating – spaghetti!

definition

A definition is the meaning of a word.

dialogue

A dialogue is a conversation between two people.

dictionary

A dictionary gives you the meanings of words. Dictionaries are arranged in alphabetical order.

diminutive

Diminutive refers to smallness. For example:

calf is the diminutive of 'cow'.

exclamation

An exclamation is a sentence which shows that we feel something strongly. It always ends with an exclamation mark. For example:

'Stop thief!' the police officer shouted.

fact

A fact is something that is true.

feminine

Some words are feminine. Some words are masculine. For example:

girl and **cow** are feminine nouns;
boy and **bull** are masculine nouns.

glossary

A glossary is a list of special words and their meanings.

headline

Headlines are the words that appear at the top of newspaper articles. They tell the reader what the story is about.

homophone

Homophones are words which sound the same but have a different meaning or different spelling. For example:

read – reed, pair – pear

hyphen

Hyphens link words together. For example:

I love freshly-baked bread.

index

An index is a list at the end of a book, telling you on which pages to find particular things.

instruction

An instruction is when we tell people to do something, or teach them how to do something

letter string

A letter string is a group of letters which occur often in words. Remembering letter strings helps us to spell. For example:

ight is a common letter string as in **light**, br**ight**, s**ight**, fr**ight**.

masculine

(See feminine)

narrator

A narrator is someone who tells a story.

negative

(See positive)

oun

noun is a naming word. It can be the name
' a person, place or thing. For example:

girl   the **park**   a **dragon**

pinion

ur opinion is what you think about something.

rder

n order is a sort of command, when you tell
meone to do something or to stop doing
mething. For example:

top making that dreadful noise!' the
acher said to the class.

aragraph

paragraph is a group of sentences that deals
ith one main idea or topic. It is easier to
ad a long piece of writing if it is divided into
iragraphs.

honeme

phoneme is the smallest unit of sound in a
ord. It may be represented by one, two,
ree or four letters. For example:

, sh**oe**, thr**ough**

phrase

A phrase is a group of words that forms part
of a sentence. Phrases are often short. They
do not usually contain a verb. Phrases do not
make sense on their own. For example:

in the night   a big footprint

plot

A plot is what happens in a story.

plural

Plural means more than one. For example:

many books

poem

A poem is a piece of writing which is
imaginative. It may express our thoughts or
feelings. It is set out in lines. The lines may or
may not rhyme.

positive

A positive word or statement is one that
means 'yes'. The opposite of positive is
negative. For example:

I can swim. (positive) I can't swim. (negative)

prefix

A prefix is a group of letters we add to the
beginning of words to change their meaning.
For example:

un as in **un**happy

preposition

A preposition is a word that tells you the position of one thing in relation to another. For example:

The cat hid **behind** the bush.

pronoun

A pronoun is a word we use instead of a noun.

Here is an example of a personal pronoun:

When Mary jumped in the puddle, **she** (Mary) got very muddy.

Here is an example of a possessive pronoun:

These are my sweets. They are **mine.**

punctuation

Punctuation helps us make sense of what we read. Punctuation marks such as full stops and commas make writing easier for us to understand.

question

A question is what we ask when we want to know something. Questions always end with a question mark. For example:

'May I stay up to watch TV?' the boy asked his mother.

rhyme

A rhyme occurs when two words have an ending that sounds the same. For example:

head, bed

rhyming couplet

A rhyming couplet is when two rhyming lines of poetry come immediately after each other. For example:

**In the dark, dark house
Lived a little grey mouse.**

rhythm

Rhythm in language is the regular pattern of beats which can be heard when the words are spoken.

root word

A root word is the smaller word from which a longer word is formed. For example:

In 'collection' the root word is **collect.**

semi-colon

A semi-colon is a punctuation mark used to separate parts of a sentence. It is stronger than a comma but not as strong as a full stop. For example:

Sam loves Indian food; Tom prefers Italian food.

setting

A setting is where a story takes place.

simile

A simile is when the writer compares the subject to something else. For example:

She was **as happy as a lark.**

ngular

ngular means that there is only one of
mething. (See plural)

peech marks

hen we write down what someone says, we
ut it inside speech marks. For example:

ne giant said, "I'm hungry."

anza

stanza is a verse or set of lines of poetry,
e pattern of which is repeated throughout
e poem.

atement

statement is a sentence that gives us
formation. For example:

ne dog ate a bone.

bject

ne subject is the main person or thing in a
ntence. For example:

ne dog barked. ('The dog' is the subject of
is sentence.)

ffix

suffix is a letter or group of letters added to
e end of a word. For example:

ider – spiders   cook – cooking

llable

onger words may be broken down into
naller parts called syllables. For example:

ad (one syllable) bad-min-ton (three syllables)

synonym

Synonyms are words with the same, or very
similar, meanings. For example:

sad, unhappy

thesaurus

A thesaurus is a book containing lists of
synonyms. The words are arranged in
alphabetical order.

title

A title is the name we give to a book, a song,
a film, a play or a picture.

verb

A verb is a doing or being word. For example:

The cat **scratched** my hand. The cat **was** angry.

verb tenses

Verbs may be written in different tenses. The
tense of the verb changes according to the
time of the action. For example:

(Present tense) Now I **am kicking** the ball.
(Past tense) Yesterday I **kicked** the ball.
(Future tense) Tomorrow I **will kick** the ball.

verse

A poem is often divided into parts, or verses.

vowel

There are five vowels in the alphabet – **a, e, i,
o, u**. Almost every word contains at least one
vowel. (See consonant)

High Frequency Word List

Term 1

ask(ed)	know
began	leave
being	might
brought	opened
can't	show
change	started
coming	stopped
didn't	think
does	thought
don't	told
found	tries
goes	turn(ed)
gone	used,
heard	walk(ed)
I'm	(ing) watch
jumped	write
knew	woke(n)

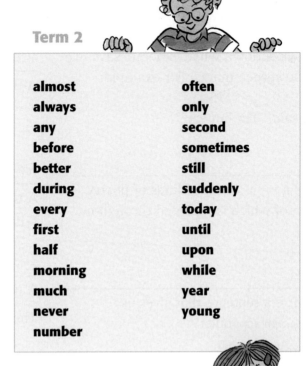

Term 2

almost	often
always	only
any	second
before	sometimes
better	still
during	suddenly
every	today
first	until
half	upon
morning	while
much	year
never	young
number	

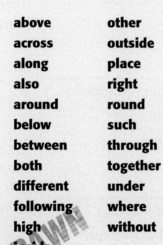

Term 3

above	other
across	outside
along	place
also	right
around	round
below	such
between	through
both	together
different	under
following	where
high	without
inside	
near	

Introduction

■ THE AUDIENCE

Language File is aimed primarily at students studying GCSE English, or Standard Grade in Scotland. It may also prove valuable to students at pre-GCSE stage, or studying language for 'A' level. In terms of the National Curriculum, it is aimed at Key Stage 4, but may be accessible to some at Key Stage 3.

■ THE BOOK AND THE TELEVISION SERIES

The book has been written in close consultation with the producers of the BBC television series of the same name. The programme titles and unit titles in the book are the same. One section of the book provides an interactive format for viewing and discussing the television programmes. Wherever possible, statements, opinions, literary and media extracts from the programmes are incorporated in the book.

■ USING THE BOOK

The ten units in the book parallel the ten programmes in the *Language File* television series. Each unit offers scope for reading a variety of texts, participating in a variety of oral activities, research, note-taking and short writing tasks. The units are arranged in three sections, each of which culminates in a substantial writing assignment suitable for an examination folder.

■ THE NATIONAL CURRICULUM

The National Curriculum in England and Wales, and its equivalent in Northern Ireland and Scotland, include Knowledge about Language as an area for study. Pages 131 and 134 of this book outline the correlation between the ten units and the Programmes of Study and Attainment Targets.

   The book is intended for use with the full ability range. It addresses itself to the issues of bilingualism, equal opportunities and multi-culturalism. The units also provide scope for focusing on language through literature, drama and the media.

   We hope, however, that this resource will do more than deliver a curriculum. We hope that it will provide opportunities for students everywhere to recognise, develop and celebrate their own unique powers of language.

Simon Fuller   Jane Joyner   David Meaden

LANGUAGE FILE

Simon Fuller

Jane Joyner

David Meaden

BBC

Longman

The authors would like to thank the following for their participation and assistance in the writing of this book:

Paul Ashton	Producer, Language File
Susie Nott-Bower	Assistant Producer
Donald Gunn	BBC Education Officer, Scotland
Peter Logue	BBC Education Officer, Northern Ireland
Rhian Watcyn Jones	BBC Senior Education Officer, Wales
Roxy Harris	ILEA Language and Literacy Unit
Angela Madge	Advisory Teacher, Hounslow
Neill Spears	Advisory Teacher, Northern Ireland
Michael Simons	ILEA English Centre
Cathy Weir	Advisory Teacher, Scotland

Feltham Hill Nursery School
Hounslow-Ealing Writing Project
West Redcar School, Cleveland

PUBLISHED BY BBC BOOKS AND LONGMAN GROUP UK LIMITED

BBC Books
a division of
BBC Enterprises Limited
Woodlands
80 Wood Lane
London W12 0TT

Longman Group UK Limited,
Longman House,
Burnt Mill,
Harlow,
Essex
CM20 2JE
England, and Associated Companies throughout the World.

First published 1990
Fourth impression 1993
© BBC Enterprises Limited/Longman Group UK Limited 1990

Cover & book design by Pep Reiff   Set in Univers Medium and Palatino
Illustrated by Mike Gilkes   Typeset by Ace Filmsetting Ltd
Cartoons by Marc Vyvyan-Jones   Text printed in Singapore

ISBN 0 582 05213 0

The Publisher's policy is to use paper manufactured from sustainable forests.

WHOSE ENGLISH?

In this unit you will investigate who owns the English Language. You will be asked to consider the part that language plays in your identity. To what extent is your language affected by where you were born, where you live, your education, your social class and your age? You will be invited to reflect on your own accent and how others react to it.

THE HARDEST THING YOU'LL EVER DO

In this unit you will investigate the ways in which we learn to talk, read and write. You will consider examples of early speech and writing as well as books offered to early readers.

You will be invited to research into your own early language development.

RINGING THE CHANGES

In this unit you will consider the enormous range of language activities that you engage in every week.

You will be invited to consider the range and purposes of reading, writing, speaking and listening.

You will be able to award yourself a certificate for the range of language that you have developed.

ASSIGNMENT 1

Using your notes from these units you will be offered a structure for writing 'A Language Autobiography'. This will be a record of your language development.

Make and keep notes on all these issues for Assignment 1.

Whose English?

SAVE THE QUEEN'S ENGLISH

DAILY Mirror

Thursday, June 29, 1989   National Sale: 3,951,601 Incorporating the Daily Record   22p

Queen's English fury as Prince attacks his staff

YOU CAN'T WRITE PROPER

ATTACK: Hard-hitting Charles who declared yesterday: "English is taught so bloody badly. The way schools are operating is not right"

And you ain't talking nice neither, says Charles

By RAMSAY SMITH, TED OLIVER, RON RICKETTS and JAMES WHITAKER

ANGRY Prince Charles yesterday branded his own staff dunces — for not writing and speaking properly.

And he said it was because English was taught so badly.

He declared: 'All the people I have in my office, they can't speak English properly, they can't write English properly.

'All the letters sent from my office I have to correct myself. And that is because English is taught so bloody badly. That is the problem.

'If we want people who write good English and write plays for the future, there is no way they can do it with the present system.

'I think the whole way schools are operating is not right. They don't rate character at all.

'I believe schools have to have discipline, furious teachers for inventing back by claiming it was civil.'

CHARLES who needed no help in the Queen's Eng...

■ Turn to Page 2

ERE! NOW KIDS DON'T 'AVE TO TALK PROPER

Schools must teach all pupils to speak and write standard English

Today
FOR A BRIGHTER TOMORROW

I am always correcting my staff's bloody bad English

Official caution

We must warn you that anything you say *or write* may be taken down and used in evidence against you.

■ LANGUAGE AND IDENTITY

The English language is a live and controversial issue, grabbing the headlines from time to time, causing people to get very worked up. It seems that language affects the way people think of themselves, and others. It seems to go hand-in-hand with a personal, a regional and a national identity.

When the English language changes, as it inevitably does, some people see it as a decline in standards, or an attack on the fabric of society. It is as if the language we all use belongs to someone else – not you or me – and we had better not play around with it, or else!

This feeling of insecurity about our own language and how we use it is reflected in these comments by British teenagers. They are talking about the way they pronounce words; their **accent.***

'You're judged by the way you talk.'
'People think we're thick because we talk kind of slow.'
'Your accent and your social status go together.'
'Sometimes you feel sort of embarrassed about your accent if you're with somebody posh.'
'Some people say our accent is degrading and it suits the city because of the unemployment.'
'If somebody said our language (Geordie) was beautiful, I would think they were taking the mickey.'

How do you feel about your accent? In your groups, discuss how different sorts of people react to the way you speak.
Do you agree or not with the statements above?

One outcome from this feeling of insecurity about how you speak is that people sometimes try to change their accent.

* Words highlighted in bold are included in the glossary.

Rita is a mature student studying Literature at the Open University. Usually, she speaks with a Liverpool accent. Frank is Rita's tutor. They have a very informal relationship and are on first-name terms.

Michael Caine and Julie Walters in a scene from Educating Rita.

FRANK *is sitting at his desk marking an essay. Occasionally he makes a tutting sound and scribbles something. There is a knock at the door.*

FRANK: Come in.

RITA *enters, closes the door, goes to the desk and dumps her bag on it. She takes her chair and places it next to* FRANK *and sits down.*

RITA *(talking in a peculiar voice)*: Hello, Frank.

FRANK *(without looking up)*: Hello. Rita, you're late.

RITA: I know, Frank. I'm terribly sorry. It was unavoidable.

FRANK *(looking up)*: Was it really? What's wrong with your voice?

RITA: Nothing is wrong with it, Frank. I have merely decided to talk properly. As Trish says there is not a lot of point in discussing beautiful literature in an ugly voice.

FRANK: You haven't got an ugly voice; at least you *didn't* have. Talk properly.

RITA: I am talking properly. I have to practise constantly, in everyday situations.

FRANK: You mean you're going to talk like that for the rest of this tutorial?

RITA: Trish says that no matter how difficult I may find it I must persevere.

FRANK: Well, will you kindly tell Trish that I am not giving a tutorial to a Dalek?

RITA: I am not a Dalek.

FRANK *(appealingly)*: Rita, stop it!

RITA: But Frank, I have to persevere in order that I shall.

FRANK: Rita! Just be yourself.

RITA *(reverting to her normal voice)*: I am being myself. *(She gets up and moves the chair back to its usual place.)*

from *Educating Rita* by Willy Russell

In your groups, discuss why Rita has decided to change the way she speaks. Is it so easy to switch from one accent to another? Why doesn't Frank like Rita changing her accent?

Whatever talking properly might mean (and Frank and Rita clearly do not agree on that) it is not about ugliness. Talk is about your identity: your class, your race and your sex. Read the next poem, 'Listen Mr Oxford don'. It is all about language and identity, about whose English we are using. Note: an Oxford don is a tutor at Oxford University.

Listen Mr Oxford don

Me not no Oxford don
me a simple immigrant
from Clapham Common
I didn't graduate
I immigrate

But listen Mr Oxford don
I'm a man on de run
and a man on de run
is a dangerous one

I ent have no gun
I ent have no knife
but mugging de Queen's English
is the story of my life

I dont need no axe
to split/   up yu syntax
I dont need no hammer
to mash/   up yu grammar

I warning you Mr Oxford don
I'm a wanted man
and a wanted man
is a dangerous one

Dem accuse me of assault
on de Oxford dictionary/
imagine a concise peaceful man like me/
dem want me serve time
for inciting rhyme to riot
but I tekking it quiet
down here in Clapham Common

I'm not a violent man Mr Oxford don
I only armed wit mih human breath
but human breath
is a dangerous weapon

So mek dem send one big word after me
I ent serving no jail sentence
I slashing suffix in self-defence
I bashing future wit present tense
and if necessary

I making de Queen's English accessory/
to my offence

John Agard

Now, in your groups, consider the following questions:
What is the 'simple immigrant' apparently doing with the English language?
Why would the poet address his poem to an Oxford don?
Why has the poet chosen to use such violent language?
Why is the poem written in a Caribbean **patois** rather than Standard English?

■ ACCENT

Our accent is important because it may tell other people a lot about us. In fact, according to American writer James Baldwin, it tells others all about us: 'To open your mouth in England is to "put your business in the street": you have confessed your parents, your youth, your school, your salary, your self-esteem, and, alas, your future.'
So why do you have the accent that you do? Here are three factors that account for your accent:

- **your place of birth, and where you have lived since**

- **your education** ● **your social class**

If you are a native English speaker you can probably tell when someone comes from America or Australia or Ireland. If you live in the British Isles, you can probably tell if a speaker comes from England, Wales, Scotland or Ireland. And within your own country, you can probably distinguish between speakers from different regions, between Fife and Edinburgh in Scotland, or between Norfolk and Lincolnshire in England, or between Bangor and Neath in Wales.

Neil Kinnock

Yvonne Murray

Caron Keating

Bob Hoskins

In your groups, can you identify your own accents?
Can you identify the accents of well-known people on television, in sport or politics?
What are the accents of the people opposite? How precise can you be?

Birthplace/domicile

● 750,000,000 people speak English
● Half this number are native speakers and half speak it as a foreign language
● 70% of all native speakers of English live in the USA
● Only 20% of native speakers of English live in the British Isles
● Many people in the British Isles have English as a second language.

■ Education

Most children who live in the British Isles attend a local school and do not change their accent during their schooldays. A small number of children go to boarding schools where they might try to alter their accent in order to talk like the others. But there are some young people who take elocution lessons to change their accent.

In the following extract from *Pygmalion* by George Bernard Shaw, Eliza Doolittle, who sells flowers on the streets of London, has come to the house of Professor Henry Higgins to learn to talk 'more genteel'. The play was first produced in 1914.

HIGGINS [*thundering*] Say your alphabet.

PICKERING. Say it, Miss Doolittle. You will understand presently. Do what he tells you ; and let him teach you in his own way.

LIZA. Oh well, if you put it like that—Ahyee, bɔyee, cɔyee, dɔyee—*

HIGGINS [*with the roar of a wounded lion*] Stop. Listen to this, Pickering. This is what we pay for as elementary education. This unfortunate animal has been locked up for nine years in school at our expense to teach her to speak and read the language of Shakespear and Milton. And the result is Ahyee, Bɔ-yee, Cɔ-yee, Dɔ-yee. [*To Eliza*] Say A, B, C, D.

LIZA [*almost in tears*] But I'm sayin it. Ahyee, Bɔyee, Cɔ-yee—

HIGGINS. Stop. Say a cup of tea.

LIZA. A cappɔtɔ-ee.

HIGGINS. Put your tongue forward until it squeezes against the top of your lower teeth. Now say cup.

LIZA. C-c-c—I cant. C-Cup.

PICKERING. Good. Splendid, Miss Doolittle.

HIGGINS.. By Jupiter, she's done it at the first shot. Pickering : we shall make a duchess of her. [*To Eliza*] Now do you think you could possibly say tea? Not tɔ-yee, mind : if you ever say bɔ-yee cɔ-yee dɔ-yee again you shall be dragged round the room three times by the hair of your head. [*Fortissimo*] T, T, T, T.

* see **phonetic spelling** in the glossary

In your groups, discuss why Eliza would want to change the way she speaks. If she learns to talk 'more genteel', what advantages and disadvantages may result? Has your school affected the way you speak?

■ Social Class

Most people in Britain speak with a regional accent. That is, an accent that is associated with a geographical place. Some people, however, speak with an accent that is referred to as 'posh', or as **Received Pronunciation (RP)**. This is the accent of a class, or group, of people. Many people associate it with South-east England, but it is spoken throughout the country by a very small percentage of the population.

Social class is difficult to define because it covers different aspects of life. It can be about your parents' jobs, about how much money you have, about social customs or leisure activities. It can be about the way you see yourself in relation to others and about the way you speak.

The chart below is one way of looking at social class. It is largely about purchasing power and is often used by advertisers to target consumers for a particular product.

Social Grade	Social status	Head of Household's Occupation
A	Upper middle class	Higher managerial, administrative or professional (e.g. Managing Director)
B	Middle class	Intermediate managerial, administrative or professional (e.g. Branch Manager of bank)
C1	Lower middle class	Supervisory or clerical, and junior managerial administrative or professional (e.g. Bank Clerk)
C2	Skilled working class	Skilled manual workers (e.g. Electrician)
D	Working class	Semi and unskilled manual workers (e.g. Cleaner)
E	Those at lowest levels of subsistence	State pensioners or widows (no other earner), casual or lowest grade worker

Look at the quotations below. Can your group match them to the social grades in the chart on the page before? How are you making your decisions? Is it what they are talking about or how they are saying it? Would it help if you could hear them? Is there anything else that you can tell about them; their gender or where they come from, for instance? You are probably not in agreement. Discuss why this is.

a) I think it's so important to wear the right things – one simply doesn't feel comfortable otherwise.

d) Well, I'm not going to bust a gut worrying about it, although I can see that chip butties may not be the best thing in the world for the old ticker.

b) Exercise? Do me a favour. I mean, how much strength does it take to lift a pint?

c) I think that environmental issues are coming more and more to the fore nationally and this will inevitably be reflected in local politics.

e) That's just blowing out money on foolishness, innit?

f) With one or two exceptions, and I mean one or two, the staff that dealt with me acted as if they thought I enjoyed being unemployed and as if it was their money that they were handing out.

■ DIALECT

As well as speaking with an accent we all speak with a **dialect**. As with accents, many people speak in a regional dialect. Others speak in **Standard English**, which is not regionally based. Many people are able to switch from Standard English to regional dialect depending on who they are with.

We distinguish between dialects by the different words and phrases each one uses. In different parts of the British Isles there are different names for everyday objects.

Do you use one of the words below, or do you use something different?

gym shoes   plimsolls   sandshoes   gutties
dappers   pumps   daps

Find out if there are other people in your group who can add different words and then spend a few minutes seeing if you can match them to areas of the country shown on the map below.

Now see how many expressions you can collect for truancy from school (e.g. 'bunking off'). You might like to think about how some of these started. There are many different types of dictionary that you can use for your research. You might look for 'bunking off' in a dictionary of slang.

■ AGE

The age we are affects our choice of words and the way we speak. New words and expressions enter the language all the time. It tends to be younger people who adopt the new words, especially **slang** or **colloquial language**. But note, this is not the same as a regional dialect. 'Tough' and 'safe', used in Programme 1, are examples of slang.

Here are some everyday expressions, or idioms. They are in use in ordinary conversation, but not always by people of all ages.

Discuss each idiom and then tick the relevant column. You may want to tick more than one column for any one idiom.

	Used in which generation?		
	MINE	**PARENTS**	**GRANDPARENTS**
Well, I'll be blowed!			
Gordon Bennett!			
Stay cool, man			
Pardon my French.			
Go on, let your hair down			
Hold your horses			
You don't know when you're well off			
We're talking megabucks			
No sweat!			
That's far out			
Wicked			
Magic			

In your group discuss how far your age influences the language you use.

■ MY LANGUAGE

Use the television programme and the activities in this unit to make notes on the following issues.

- Where you were born and how that has affected the way you speak.

- Whether you have moved and if that has altered the way you speak.

- How your education may have affected the way you speak.

- Whether your accent reflects your social class.

- Whether you vary your accent at all.

- Whether or not you speak in a regional dialect, Standard English, a patois, and if you vary your dialect according to the person you are talking to.

- Whether you have another language that affects when and where you speak English.

- Whether the way you speak reflects your age.

- Whether or not you could change the way you speak, and why?

- The unit title, 'Whose English?', suggests that English belongs to somebody. Do you feel it is your language – or someone else's?

Keep these notes. You will need them at the end of this part of the book when you write your assignment.

The Hardest Thing You'll Ever Do

■ LEARNING TO TALK

The first sounds you made were probably the screams of a hungry or unhappy baby. At about two months old you probably started gurgling and babbling, because you were happy or were being fed!

All this activity prepared your vocal chords for saying your first words, although you would not have realised that. The development of vocabulary would have been very rapid. Look at Eddie's progress, as recorded by his mother:

> **8 months: dadadada . . . nananana . . .**
> **9 months: godley . . . godley**
> **12 months: dukths (ducks), busth (bus)**
> **17 months: hoover, cheese, marmite**

From one-word utterances, you would have progressed to two and have learned about word order. Here's Eddie again:

> **19 months: fankoo (thank you)**
> **22 months: down dare (down there), man . . . ladder (pointing)**

Over the next two years you would have learnt that language has a social function. It enables you to interact with the world. For example:

Language gets things done: 'Mummy, come here.'
Language tells the world about you: 'I rided my trike.'
Language can be imaginative: 'Eddie driving bin lorry.'
Language can discover things: 'Why?'

By the age of four or five, you would have acquired about a 2,000-word vocabulary, taught yourself the rules of **grammar** and **syntax** and would be able to hold conversations with people.

Quite remarkable, isn't it?

There is no such thing as an average child. However, if there was, its speech and language development might look like this:

Age 0–2 months
Discomfort sounds

Age 2–4 months
Add pleasure sounds

Age 4–9 months
Babbling

Age 9–18 months
Building sound system

Age 18 months–2½ years
Two-word phrases

Age 2½–4 years
Learn grammar, expand vocabulary
Complete sound system

Age 4–6 years
Adult grammar and syntax

■ LEARNING THE RULES

When you learnt to talk you would have made a lot of mistakes. It is part of the learning process. At first, your parents probably thought it funny, but after a while they probably started correcting you, or trying to.

There is a lot of evidence which suggests that you are born with the ability to work out the rules of language for yourself without being told. When young children say, 'I *runned* down the road' or 'I *eated* the apple', it is not because they have heard someone say it but because they have worked out for themselves that we usually add -ed to show that something has already happened.

e.g.	Present Tense	Past Tense
	walk	walked
	hop	hopped

We should really be congratulating them for what they have achieved rather than telling them that they have got it wrong because, in this particular case, the rule does not apply.

i.e.	Present Tense	Past Tense
	run	ran
	eat	ate

Timothy has learnt from experience that we usually add -s to show that there is more than one of something (plural) and, on hearing 'hoax', has assumed that this is *hoaks* and means more than one *hoak* – a word which does not exist. Although he is factually wrong, he has had to learn a lot in order to make this mistake.

It is only through experimenting and making mistakes that we can develop our understanding of language, although the number of mistakes will decrease as we become more experienced users.

> Ask someone who knew you when you were very young about the sorts of things that you said when you were experimenting with language.
>
> If you have the opportunity, listen to some young children and make a note of the ways in which they use language. You might find it easier to tape record them and then **transcribe** the recording.

■ LEARNING TO READ

Can you remember how you learnt to read? It is something that happens gradually, over a long period of time. Perhaps you can remember some of the books you used when you first started school? Maybe you still have books at home which were favourites when you were very young?

Ideas about how we learn to read have changed a lot in the last fifty years. Now people realise that learning to read is a lot like learning to talk. You learn both things by doing them. You do not learn to read by practising separate sounds but by reading interesting books with a person who reads well.

Fifty years ago someone might have tried to teach a young child to read by saying,

'c . . . a . . . t spells cat'

and saying the sound of every letter. But of course this wouldn't work with words like 'newt' and 'budgerigar'.

The poem below makes fun of a certain kind of book that used to be used to teach children to read. The strange style it is written in is to be found in many reading schemes. It is intended to help children to read but it is actually a very boring and extremely unnatural style. The poem also ridicules the sexism of some reading schemes.

Reading Scheme

Here is Peter. Here is Jane. They like fun.
Jane has a big doll. Peter has a ball.
Look, Jane, look! Look at the dog! See him run!

Here is Mummy. She has baked a bun.
Here is the milkman. He has come to call.
Here is Peter. Here is Jane. They like fun.

Go, Peter! Go, Jane! Come, milkman, come!
The milkman likes Mummy. She likes them all.
Look, Jane, look! Look at the dog! See him run!

Here are the curtains. They shut out the sun.
Let us peep! On tiptoe, Jane! You are small!
Here is Peter. Here is Jane. They like fun.

I hear a car, Jane. The milkman looks glum.
Here is Daddy in his car. Daddy is tall.
Look, Jane, look! Look at the dog! See him run!

Daddy looks very cross. Has he a gun?
Up, milkman! Up, milkman! Over the wall!
Here is Peter. Here is Jane. They like fun.
Look, Jane, look! Look at the dog! See him run!

Wendy Cope

Now we do not talk about teaching reading, but about helping children to learn to read.

In pairs discuss this list of things that a parent or guardian could do to help a child to learn to read. Rearrange the list into an order of importance, missing out any you think would not help at all. Note down your order and compare it with another pair's order.

a) **buy lots of interesting books**
b) **read out loud to the child**
c) **point out writing for the child to read, e.g. signs, labels**
d) **join the local library**
e) **encourage the child to ask questions about what is read**
f) **pick books with good pictures**
g) **choose funny books**
h) **read the same books lots of times**
i) **let the child choose the books to be read**
j) **ask the child to retell the story using the book**

Becoming a reader is so much more than just working out what the marks on a page say. It is about getting pleasure from reading, choosing books, knowing which way up to hold a book and how to turn the pages and fitting what you read in the book to the knowledge you already have of the world. It is possible to begin to become a reader from about the age of one, when some children are already getting pleasure from books as well as holding them the right way up!

The final stage of becoming a reader is moving from dependence on someone who can read (a parent or a teacher, for example) to independence, when the child reads alone. At first the child reads out loud but gradually reading becomes silent until the words become thoughts in the brain. Of course we go on learning to be better readers all our lives as we read a greater variety of things in different ways (see the next unit).

Ask people who can remember you when you were very young to tell you about how you learnt to read and which books you enjoyed most. Make notes of what they say; you will need them at the end of this section.

Excellent books for young children have been published in recent years, as a visit to a bookshop or library will prove. The best combine interesting illustrations, natural and imaginative language and a powerful story which repays many reads. Here is an example:

Later on, the Postman,
  Feeling hot,
Came upon a 'grandma' in a shady spot;
  But 'Grandma'
What big *teeth* you've got!

Besides, this is a letter for . . . Oooh!

URGENT

B. B. Wolf Esq.
C/o Grandma's Cottage
Horner's Corner

MEENY, MINY, MO & CO., SOLICITORS
Alley O Buildings, Toe Lane, Tel: 12345.

Dear Mr Wolf,

We are writing to you on behalf of our client, Miss Riding-Hood, concerning her grandma. Miss Hood tells us that you are presently occupying her grandma's cottage and wearing her grandma's clothes without this lady's permission.

Please understand that if this harassment does not cease, we will call in the Official Woodcutter, and - if necessary - all the King's horses and all the King's men.

On a separate matter, we must inform you that Messrs. Three Little Pigs Ltd. are now firmly resolved to sue for damages. Your offer of shares in a turnip or apple-picking business is declined, and all this huffing and puffing will get you nowhere.

Yours sincerely,

Harold Meeny

H Meeny

from *The Jolly Postman* by Janet and Allan Ahlberg

■ LEARNING TO WRITE

Can you remember when you first began to write? As with talking and reading, it is a gradual process and it is difficult to say at which point you were actually producing what most people would recognise as writing.

You certainly started making marks on paper when you were very young, and once you began to understand that the funny marks in books actually meant something, you may well have started making marks and squiggles of your own. You were probably able to 'read' these squiggles to other people, although you might have forgotten what they meant soon afterwards.

You then started using a mixture of pictures and scribbles that began to look more like letters. Your name was probably the first word that you learnt to recognise and copy and you then went on to recognise other words that used some of the same letters.

You continued to experiment and at first you ran words together and used a mixture of capital and small letters (lower case), and you invented a lot of spellings. Gradually you began to spell words in the accepted way and it became easier for other people to read.

Through continued experimenting and greater familiarity with different sorts of books, comics and TV programmes you became more confident and began to use full stops, capital letters and other punctuation. This process of experimenting with writing and meeting new forms can continue right through your adult life.

Ask if anyone at home has kept any of your early writing. Does it look as if you tried to imitate the shapes of words on a page? What is the earliest example of your writing your own name? If you are able to, compare your writing with others in your group.

Can you remember how you felt about writing when you went to school for the first time? You probably did handwriting exercises until you could form your letters properly. Were you encouraged to write freely or did you copy a lot of things from the board? When your teachers looked at your writing, what did they comment on first:

>   what you were trying to say?
>   the neatness of your handwriting?
>   the spelling and word order?

In your group compare your answers to the last question and discuss the order of importance in which you would place these three aspects of writing.

■ MY EARLY LANGUAGE

Make sure you have notes on the following:

- What have you found about your earliest efforts at talking? Can you remember things you said or things that others said to you about your speech?

- What memories do you have of being read to and of your own early reading? Do you remember your favourite books or stories? Do you remember reading other things, like signs?

- What do you remember of your early writing? Have you any examples of it to include in your language history? What kinds of writing did you enjoy, if any?

- Who have been the judges of the way you read, write and talk? Have they been fair judges?

Keep these notes. You will need them at the end of this part of the book when you write your assignment.

Ringing the Changes

■ THE PEOPLE YOU TALK TO

Here is a list of some of the people that it might be possible to talk to and listen to at home:

parents | friends
siblings | neighbours
baby siblings | pets (not people, but they do get talked to!)
other relatives

> Make your own list of all the kinds of people you talk to or listen to at school.

You do not speak to all these people in the same way. It is unlikely that when your father says, 'Come and help me with the washing-up', you will reply, 'Yes, sir.' It is equally unlikely that when your headteacher asks, 'Are you in the fifth year?' you will reply, 'You must be joking!' We all change the way we speak depending on whom we are speaking to.

Sometimes we just change the tone of voice, for example people often sound different when they are saying hello to babies and toddlers. Their voices are often softer, gentler and more friendly.

Sometimes we change the vocabulary. When talking to very young children some people use some very odd words that they would not use with anyone else, e.g. horsey, doggy, biccy. People sometimes try to use difficult vocabulary and unusual words with someone they are trying to impress.

Accent and dialect are often changed when people are trying to impress. At a job interview most people will try to speak Standard English; this may be with their own accents but most people will attempt to make their accents sound like one you might hear on the BBC.

◼ LANGUAGE AND POWER

Another factor that affects the way you speak is the power relationship between you and the person you are talking with.

When you are talking with your parents, or other adults, they are usually in the powerful position. Below is an extreme example of a parent exerting power; it was written by a thirteen-year-old girl using some of her mother's favourite expressions.

Don't Interrupt

Turn the television down!
None of your cheek!
Sit down!
Shut up!
Don't make a fool of yourself!
Respect your elders!
Don't walk so fast!
Don't run!
Don't interrupt when I'm talking!

Don't forget to brush your teeth!
Don't forget to polish your shoes!
Don't slam the door!
Go to your room!
Don't shout!
Don't stuff yourself with sweets!
Don't point!
Don't listen to my conversation!
Don't interrupt me when I'm talking!

Demetroulla Vassili

Power relationships continue down through the family.

Draw, using stick people if you like, a similar set of cartoons showing how power is demonstrated in the use of language in school.

THE RANGE OF WRITING

This is a formality scale, onto which it would be possible to plot the different range of writing we are likely to encounter.

very formal . . . . . . formal . . . . . . informal . . . . very informal
1 . . . 2 . . . 3 . . . 4 . . . 5 . . . 6 . . . 7 . . . 8 . . . 9 . . . 10

An invitation to a royal garden party would be written in a very formal style, so it would appear on the extreme left of the scale.

A note to a best friend would be very informal and it would appear on the extreme right of the scale.

> Discuss in your groups where the following pieces of writing would fit on the formality scale:
>
> **a note to yourself to remember something**
> **a note to the person who delivers the milk**
> **a school report**
> **a newspaper article**
> **a poem**
> **a shopping list**
> **a letter explaining absence from school**
> **a birth certificate**

Writing is similar to talking and listening, in that we match purpose, topic and audience to the range of writing we produce.

Here is a list of some of the range of writing you could do at home:

lists
letters
diaries
notes
messages
homework (stories, reports, discursive writing, etc.)
poems
advertisements

Make your own list of the range or writing you would cover at school.

Your list should be quite long. As with talking, your writing will vary from quick, informal bits (for example, notes to yourself) to much more formal, finished pieces (for example, an assignment that is part of an examination course or a letter of application for a job).

People at school (especially in their final years!) are expected to produce enormous amounts of writing of different kinds. Most adults do not do a great deal of writing unless they choose to, or have jobs that require it.

Make a note of all the different kinds of writing you do in a typical week. The best way would be to begin now to note down everything you write over the next seven days. Or you could look back over last week and try to remember everything you wrote. Add this to your list of writing done in school.

For homework ask at least one adult to do the same thing.

When you have both sets of notes compare them and you will probably find that the adult does very little writing of any length during the week.

■ SO MUCH TO READ

Have you ever stopped to think about all the reading the average person does in a day? Starting with the cereal packet at breakfast and the names and addresses on any letters that may arrive the list could include:

instructions
labels
comics, magazines
books
newspapers
letters, postcards
messages, notes
recipes
road signs
record covers

and you could probably think of more.

All these items are read for very different purposes and in very different ways. A recipe has to be read closely and carefully, otherwise what is being made could turn out to be inedible. The same is true of instructions; you do not want your self-assembly table to collapse. You may find yourself reading out loud if you are particularly keen to get something right. You are skim reading when you read something superficially to get a general impression. This is probably the way you would read your school report, on a first reading.

If you are looking in a reference book to find a particular piece of information, for example what lizards eat, you will use several different kinds of reading. You will probably start off by scanning the L section of the index to find what page information about lizards is on. Scanning is when you are looking for something in particular, and you half read things until you spot what you are looking for.

Having seen lizard you will look up the page number and when you have located the section about lizards you will then read it very closely and carefully, in order to find out all you can about what they eat. You may even read some particularly useful bits two or three times to make sure that you have understood them.

Why do we read? This is an interesting question to which the answer is, it depends on who we are and what we are reading.

List all the things you can remember reading in the last week. Now group them according to why you read them (was it for pleasure, because someone told you to, for information, or for another reason?). You may find that some things would fit into more than one group. Write, as a heading for each group, the reason for reading, e.g.:

For Information

Street map
Booklet that came with new camera
Writing at base of statue by Town Hall

What some people do not realise about reading is that the meaning of a piece of writing is made in a slightly different way by each individual reader. Meaning is not contained within print. Because each reader is a different person, coming to the print with different experiences and knowledge, each reader will make a different meaning. To test this out read the passage below:

Kate strode along the path high up on the Pembrokeshire cliff. She was resolute, she would support Henry against Richard. Her eyes scanned the horizon for Henry's boat but the grey mist prevented her from seeing more than a few hundred yards. Kittiwakes called their names from the cliffs below her and thrift dotted the slopes above.

In pairs discuss what this passage is about, what kind of book it comes from and what might happen next.

You may have known what kittiwakes are. If you did not, they are sea birds that nest on cliffs. They got their name from their call, which sounds like 'kittiwake'. Thrift is a plant which grows in clumps and has a pale purple flower.

If this was new knowledge discuss how it alters your reading of the passage.

Did you know what 'resolute' means? If not it could have meant 'happy' or 'sad' and therefore the whole meaning of the passage would have altered. It means 'determined' or 'decided'.

If you were not sure what it meant discuss your new reading now you do know.

Finally, and it is unlikely that anyone using this book will have brought this knowledge to a first reading of the passage, Henry refers to the man who became Henry VII. He sailed from France, landed in South Wales and went on to defeat King Richard III in 1485.

In pairs, read the passage again with all this new knowledge. Now discuss what this passage is about, what kind of book it comes from and what you think might happen next.

Your final reading should have been very different from your first reading. You can probably see now how the same bit of writing can be read differently depending on what the reader brings to it. The meaning is not contained within the print.

Who reads what and why?
Pick three from the list of books described below that you think you might like to read. Work in a pair so that you can discuss items on the list whilst making your individual choices.

a horror story
a horror story written one hundred years ago
a description of someone's journey to the North Pole
short stories written by a young woman
short stories written by an old man
a novel set in World War One
the diary of a woman set in World War One
a long novel about rich film stars in Hollywood
a play about a group of teenagers
a poetry anthology
a love story
a love story written one hundred years ago
a thriller
science fiction stories
the autobiography of a famous person
a book of comic verse
a novel by Shirley Conran
a novel by Charles Dickens

This exercise should have made it clear that you have developed a strong personal preference. You probably like some types of books (genres) more than others. You may look out for particular authors you enjoy and make a point of avoiding others. What determines this? Have you copied the reading habits of someone you admire? Do you read certain books because your friends read them? Have you ever tried books of the kind you say you don't like? Does your gender determine what you like to read?

Have a discussion in your group about how people's tastes in books are formed. Make notes of any points that interest you. After the discussion add to your notes by reflecting on how your own tastes were formed.

CERTIFICATE

for exceptional speaking/listening, reading and writing and for ringing the changes.

This is to certify that

....

has spoken and listened to

adults (teachers and family), children, babies, animals, self, etc, in order to communicate, persuade, amuse, inform, instruct, express emotion, etc.

has read

lists, letters, novels, cereal packets, newspapers, magazines, short stories, comics, poems, road signs, etc, for information, pleasure, direction, edification and delight.

has written

stories, reports, letters, diaries, notes, descriptions, poems, plays, etc, so as to clarify understanding, demonstrate knowledge, inform, amuse, etc.

■ ASSIGNMENT 1
A language autobiography

By now you should have many notes from the first three units of this book. Look back through them. You should have notes from 'Whose English?' about your accent and dialect and issues related to how you speak. Check back to the last page of that unit for details.

You should have notes from the unit called 'The Hardest Thing' about how you learnt to talk, read and write. Check back to the last page of that unit for details.

On the page before this is a certificate which could be awarded to you. The certificate is designed to show you that, regardless of whether you think you are good at English or not, you can talk, read and write in a wide variety of ways for a wide range of purposes. You will have made notes in the course of the chapter on all the specific things you have done.

Using all these notes plan an assignment called 'A Language Autobiography' in which you will discuss the influences on your language from when you were a baby until now. Make sure your opinions are included in the writing as well as facts.

There are many ways that such an assignment could be structured:
- chronologically – describing and reflecting on things in the order in which they happened
- in order of importance – starting with what you consider to have been the most important influence on your language, for example, how you may have moved house to a place where your accent and dialect were laughed at.
- looking back – discussing how you feel about your language now and reflecting on how it was influenced during the course of your life.

When you have planned your assignment discuss the plan with people in your group before you begin to write your rough draft. When your rough draft is complete get as many people as possible to read it and take their views into account when you redraft. In this way your final draft should be as good as you can make it.

TALKING PROPER

In this unit you will be asked to consider the variety of accents used today and the status of Received Pronunciation.

You will also be asked to consider the difference between Standard English and regional dialects and the history and status of Standard English. You will reflect on whether you are 'talking proper'.

STICKS AND STONES

In this unit you will examine the issue of swear words and their use in books and on television and consider racist and sexist language.

You will also consider subjects that are regarded as taboo by different sections of society and how we use language to avoid talking about them directly.

TRYING TO CONNECT YOU

In this unit you will find out about the spread of the English language in the nineteenth century.

You will consider the achievement of people in Britain today who can speak more than one language and find out how schools support bilingualism.

ASSIGNMENT 2

Using your notes from these three units you will be able to write A School Language Policy, which takes account of language diversity and looks at what 'talking proper' means. You will also consider how offensive language might be dealt with.

Make and keep notes on all these issues for Assignment 2.

Talking Proper

■ ACCENTS

. . . Throw the 'R' away

I've been so sad
Since you said my accent was bad
He's worn a frown
This Caledonian clown
I'm just going to have to learn to hesitate
To make sure my words
On your Saxon ears don't grate
But I wouldn't know a single word to say
If I flattened all the vowels
And threw the 'R' away . . .

The Proclaimers

Like The Proclaimers, most people have been told at some time in their lives that they don't speak properly. It is not a very pleasant experience. The way we pronounce words is called our accent. We all speak with an accent, but some accents would appear to be more acceptable than others. The Proclaimers speak with a Scots accent.

A few people don't speak with a regional accent, but with an accent called Received Pronunciation (RP). This accent is often described as 'posh' because it is an accent associated with a particular class of people.

What accent do you speak with? Do your friends and classmates all have the same accent?

What do you mean by 'talking posh'? Who, in your view, talks posh?

Do you use phrases like 'talking common' or 'talking normal'? If so, who do you think talks in that way?

If you want to show that someone is talking with an accent when you are writing, you can do so by using certain spellings and punctuation marks.

1 'Even just sitn doonin writn, a don't no that am sayn whut a mean.'
2 'Ever' man was ma frien' when a' lef – an' now ah've come back to mah frien's.'
3 'Are you goin' ter gi'e me ony bloody tea?'
4 'Nah, a dahn't fink 'e's gonna 'ave time ta do it.'
5 'See our Billy, he thinks yous not wise.

Read these sentences aloud to each other. Can you identify the accents? Which one is Texas, Nottingham, Glasgow, London or Northern Ireland?

Now try reading aloud the following representation of a very posh accent:

'Sway thing, Kleddies n Gentlemen, the chew-lolla gree with mih whennay seh, femmay coiner phrezz, we raw linner grimment. A nah wesher losk Leddie Mogretto, hosh lair sair, to sephew words.' (from *Fraffly Suite* by A. Lauder)

Here is a 'translation':

'So I think, Ladies and Gentlemen, that you'll agree with me when I say, if I may coin a phrase, we are all in agreement. And now we shall ask Lady Margaret, how shall I say, to say a few words.'

Today, some people think that if you do not speak with an RP accent you are not talking properly. They may write letters to newspapers or phone in to radio programmes.

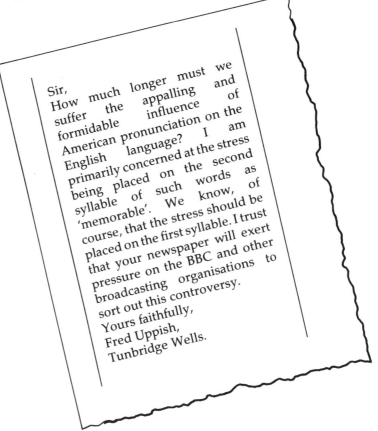

Sir,
How much longer must we suffer the appalling and formidable influence of American pronunciation on the English language? I am primarily concerned at the stress being placed on the second syllable of such words as 'memorable'. We know, of course, that the stress should be placed on the first syllable. I trust that your newspaper will exert pressure on the BBC and other broadcasting organisations to sort out this controversy.
Yours faithfully,
Fred Uppish,
Tunbridge Wells.

How would you pronounce these three words that appear in the above letter? The mark shows where to place the stress.

fórmidable or formídable

cóntroversy or contróversy

prímarily or primárily

In your group discuss why people write this sort of letter. Is it concern about pronunciation or class or what?

Concern about correct pronunciation is quite recent. In the last century many well-known and powerful people felt no need to change their regional accent. Sir Robert Peel, Conservative Prime Minister from 1841–1846, spoke with a Midlands accent, despite his education at Harrow School and Oxford University. William Gladstone was Liberal Prime Minister four times between 1868 and 1894. Again, although educated at Eton School and Oxford University, he spoke with a Lancashire accent.

'Bostin, Bill.'

'Eh up, Bob, ow's it goin'?'

Sir Robert Peel

Sir William Gladstone

Do you think it matters what accent a Prime Minister of today has?

As well as believing that regional accents are incorrect, some people argue that they are ugly, sloppy and ineffective.

You might like to test your own attitudes to accents by answering these questions as honestly as possible.

1 A new student arrives in your class speaking with a completely different accent from everyone else.

Would you: (a) make fun of the accent by mimicking whatever the student said?

(b) ignore the student and his/her weird accent?

(c) treat the student like anyone else?

2 You win a competition and spend a day with a famous TV personality who speaks 'posh' and comments on your accent.

Would you: (a) ignore the remark and change the subject?

(b) explain what you know about the variety of accents used around the English-speaking world?

(c) subtly alter the way you speak?

3 You are going for a job interview.

Would you: (a) act naturally and speak as you always do?

(b) speak as normal but use the appropriate sort of language for an interview?

(c) alter your accent?

Discuss in your group what conclusions you might draw from your answers.

■ DIALECTS

Like accents, dialects are usually described by the region from which they come. We might refer to a Berkshire dialect, or a Northumberland dialect. Most people who speak in a regional dialect also speak with a regional accent, but accent and dialect are not the same. Each person speaks with an accent, but many people can switch from one dialect to another, depending on whom they are talking to. If you have been watching the television programmes, you will have heard Billy Kay, who speaks with a Scots accent, switch between Standard English and an Ayrshire dialect.

A dialect has three main features: grammar, vocabulary, accent. That is to say that dialects:

- have different rules governing the way words and sentences are put together (grammar)
- use some words that no other dialect uses (vocabulary)
- tend to be spoken in a regional accent. Scouse (Liverpool), Geordie (Newcastle), Cockney (London) or Ulster (Northern Ireland) are usually thought of as accents as well as dialects.

Can you name any other dialects, particularly ones spoken in your area?
Can you recall any particular words or phrases of those dialects?

Sometimes regional dialects are referred to as non-standard, because they are being compared to Standard English. This makes them seem as if they are incorrect, or inadequate. This is not so. But it is the case that Standard English has a greater status than any other dialect. It tends to be the language of Parliament, the law courts, schools, colleges and universities.

■ STANDARD ENGLISH

- Standard English is used for almost all writing (except where the writer is deliberately using a non-standard form).
- Standard English is used for speaking on radio and TV (except in dramas or soaps where characters deliberately speak in dialect).
- Standard English can be spoken with any regional accent (e.g. Dorset) or any national accent (e.g. Welsh).

But Standard English is a relatively new idea. Its rules, or grammar, have only gradually evolved since the Middle Ages.

Look at some of the changes:

> The word 'silly' meant 'empty' 200 years ago. It has also meant 'innocent', 'unworldly', 'foolish'. Now it means 'stupid'.
> New words are constantly entering the language, like 'glasnost' from the USSR, 'movie' from the USA, 'tandoori' from India and 'reggae' from Jamaica.

The influence of new technology is also considerable. For example, the word 'wireless' has been replaced by 'radio'. But when part of a hi-fi unit it is called a tuner. CB radio enthusiasts would refer to a receiver.

The point is, Standard English is not a fixed entity. It is changing as new words and phrases enter the language. As these words are increasingly used, they find their way into dictionaries and become part of the written as well as the spoken language.

To understand how one particular regional dialect came to be regarded as 'Standard English', you need to know a little about the history of language in Britain.

■ A BRIEF HISTORY OF STANDARD ENGLISH

The Celts invade from Europe. They speak Celtic. Some of their words have entered the English language (e.g. crag, combe = valley).

The Romans invade Britain. They rule for 400 years. Many British place-names have Latin origin (e.g. Duoverum = Dover).

With the invasions of Angles and Saxons, Danes and Vikings, Celtic continues to flourish only in Scotland and Ireland. The Britons, called Wealas (Welsh), are driven west. 'Old English' becomes the main language, with its three or four major dialects.

Here is an example of 'Old English', with a modern translation.

Syle me aenne hafoc.
Ic sylle lustice, gyf þu
sylst me aenne stwiftne hund.

Give me a hawk.
I give one willingly, if you give me a fast dog.

The Normans invade. French becomes the language of the court. The mass of people still speak 'Old English'. Many French words are adopted by English speakers: e.g. mayor, prince, minister, beef and mutton. Latin is still used by scholars. English is first introduced into Ireland.

The mixing of French and 'Old English' produces 'Middle English'. This is the language of Geoffrey Chaucer, a London civil servant, who writes *The Canterbury Tales* in 1387. At the time there is no agreement on rules of syntax or of spelling. Chaucer's spelling reflects the pronunciation of his London dialect.
In Scotland, English, called Scots, develops its own national standard and literary tradition.

Its main influences are Northumbrian English and Gaelic, the original language of the Scots.

Welsh is still the major language in Wales, and Irish in Ireland.

Here is an extract from Chaucer's 'The Pardoner's Tale' with a modern translation.

And with that word it happed him, par cas,	And with those words, it happened, by chance,
To take the botel ther the poysoun was,	that he took the bottle with the poison in it,
And drank and yaf his felawe drynke also	and he drank and gave his friend a drink also,
For which anon they storren bothe two.	which is why they both died instantly.

1476

Caxton's Press

William Caxton sets up a printing press in London. He uses the local dialect, East Midlands, as the standard form for all the books. This dialect is used in an area that includes the universities of Oxford and Cambridge and the City of London, centre of law and government. The East Midlands dialect reflects the power of a region and of a class of people.

1600 ~ 1800

The pattern of a written standard form is set by Caxton. Increasing standardisation in spelling and grammar through the Bible, dictionaries and grammar books establishes the written form of Standard English used today throughout the British Isles. The status of Scots is undermined by the Union of Crowns, 1603, and Parliaments, 1707, and the spread of the English Bible. English spreads into Wales and Ireland through the influence of the Bible and English landowners.

1800 — 1922

The Rain in Spain falls Mainly on the Plain!

BBC

The term 'Standard English' is now used with reference to speech. The efforts of the new middle class to establish a 'polite' way of speaking are reinforced by the Public Schools, the Civil Service, and later by the BBC. The accent known as Received Pronunciation (RP) is associated with a middle class largely based in South-East England.

■ STANDARD ENGLISH AND REGIONAL DIALECTS

There are many similarities between Standard English and regional dialects, but here are some of the differences:

- Some dialects have kept forms that are no longer used in Standard English (e.g. 'thee', 'tha' in Yorkshire, 'feard' in Northern Ireland).
- Some dialects have words that have never been part of Standard English (e.g. 'frit' instead of frightened, in Norfolk).
- Many English dialects, like the French language, use a double negative in a sentence (e.g. 'I didn't pay for no chips.' In Standard English that would be: 'I didn't pay for any chips.').
- Many dialects keep a regular verb form, where Standard English varies. For example, dialects: 'I was . . . we was', or 'I were . . . we were', but Standard English: 'I was . . . we were.'

Here are some examples of dialect:

1 'Look after the wains' (Belfast).
2 'Us get used to it' (Devon).
3 'She get on well now' (Suffolk).
4 'He was betterer than me' (West Yorkshire).
5 'I lived there for eight year' (Carlisle).
6 'I've no seen the bairn' (Scotland).
7 'She do like reading' (South Wales).

In your group, discuss how the dialect forms are different from Standard English.

■ CREOLES

So, in Britain today, we have a number of dialects being spoken alongside Standard English. We also have the Afro-Caribbean **creole** languages. In the Caribbean these languages developed from the early days of slavery, when slaves from different cultures were forced suddenly to live together. They developed a language that was a mix of other languages and English. This is called a **pidgin**. The pidgin developed into a mother tongue and became a creole.

Like any dialect, a creole is rule-based. It does not have some arbitrary grammar as some people think. Here are some key differences between Caribbean Creole and Standard English:

Louise Bennett

- Creole nouns do not add 's' in the plural ('Eight girl swim in the race.')
- Creole does not use the ''s' but 'fi' to show possession.
    ('Michael's hat' becomes 'fi Michael hat'.)
- Creole does not alter verb endings to show singular/plural or tense.
    ('Jane live near me. She walk home last night.')
- Creole uses multiple negatives.
    ('Nobody no buy no present for you.')
- Creole does not alter the word order for questions.
    ('What time it is?')
- Creole makes much use of duplication and repetition, especially in storytelling.

On the next page is a transcript from a talk by the poet Louise Bennett on the language of Jamaica.

Jamaica derive!

Like my Auntie Roachy say she vex any time she hearing the people a come style fi we Jamaica language as 'corruption of the English language'.

You ever hear anything go so? Aunt Roachy she say she no know why mek dem no call the English language corruption of the Norman French and the Greek and the Latin where they say English is derived from. Oonu hear the word: English 'derive' but Jamaica 'corrupt.

No, massa, nothing no go so. We not corrupt and them derive. We derive, too. Jamaica derive!

> Working in pairs, try to list some of the differences between the language of this passage and Standard English.

■ SLANG AND DIALECT

When it comes to writing, Standard English is the norm. But it can be very effective and good fun to introduce dialect and slang. Compare these two versions of Little Red Riding Hood. The first is written in Standard English. The second version has been written by students from West Redcar School, County Cleveland, incorporating local slang and dialect.

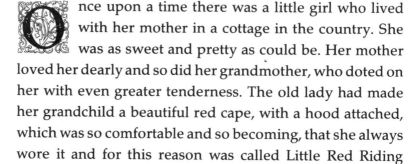

Once upon a time there was a little girl who lived with her mother in a cottage in the country. She was as sweet and pretty as could be. Her mother loved her dearly and so did her grandmother, who doted on her with even greater tenderness. The old lady had made her grandchild a beautiful red cape, with a hood attached, which was so comfortable and so becoming, that she always wore it and for this reason was called Little Red Riding Hood.

One morning the mother said to her daughter, 'Come, Little Red Riding Hood, take this basket to your grandmother. She has been ill and . . .'

onks ago there lived a young bairn who lived with her mam in a cottage in the country. She was the bonniest wooliback in the county. Her mam loved her a lot and so did her biddy of a nana who doted on her with great tenderness. Her old biddy had made her kidder a gorge red cape with a hood, which was so comfy and so cadj, that she always wore it, so they called her Little Red Riding Hood.

One morning the mam said to her little bairn, ' 'Ere, take this basket to yer nan. She's been borking all over the joint so . . .'

wooliback . . . country person   gorge . . . gorgeous
cadj . . . smart   borking . . . sick

Try writing a version of a fairy tale using your own local dialect and slang.

Now answer these questions and make notes

1 When do you use Standard English in conversation and when do you use a non-standard form? Make a list of situations and who you are talking to in each case.
2 How many different ways can you speak?
3 Do you always write in Standard English? When would you not?
4 What is going on in your school? Is your accent or dialect equally accepted by all teachers and students? Do you feel pressured to change?
5 What's your attitude to Standard English?
   Is it (a) the correct way to speak and write?
        (b) useful if you can handle it but not essential?
        (c) absolutely necessary, especially in public life?
        (d) just another English dialect of English?
6 Are you 'talking proper'?

Keep the notes from your discussion for the assignment at the end of this part of the book.

Sticks and Stones

'Sticks and stones may break my bones
But words shall never hurt me'

Is this old saying true? Words may not be able to cause any physical harm but they can certainly hurt your feelings. You may suffer abuse because of your race, your colour, your religion, your gender, your class, your physical appearance or even your age.

Many of the words used to abuse people are what we call swearwords. They are also sometimes called expletives or obscenities. Most people use them on some occasions. Prince Charles recently said that the reason he had to correct letters sent from his office was, 'because English is taught so *bloody* badly'.

In writing this book we experienced some difficulty with these sorts of words. Although almost everyone has heard them spoken and seen them written down in some books, or more commonly as graffiti, many people would object to them being printed, especially in a book designed to be used in schools.

There are a number of ways of getting around this problem. Some news-papers will print the initial letter of the word followed by a series of dashes, e.g. s———! Others might use a string of symbols, like this: *#≠‡§¿!

US President Richard Nixon made recordings of conversations with various officials in his White House office. These were later to become known as the Watergate Tapes, and when transcripts were published the swearwords were removed and replaced by the expression 'expletive deleted'.

Another way around the problem is to substitute a different word. In the following extract from the popular TV comedy series 'Porridge', it is not hard to guess which word 'naff' is replacing.

BARROWCLOUGH   Fletcher, a new arrival is moving in here and that's
                that, so you may as well accept it as a fait accompli.
                He leaves and Fletcher crosses to the door.
HARRIS   I'll be off too then, Fletch. Bit crowded in here. I hope
                the three of you will be very happy.
FLETCHER   Naff off, Harris.
HARRIS   Naff off yourself, Fletch. With knobs on.

If people swear on the radio or television the offending word is often replaced by an electronic sound or 'bleep'. On some 'live' phone-in radio programmes there is actually a few seconds delay built into the transmission so that someone who starts swearing can be cut off.

Teachers are often asked by their students if they can use swearwords in their writing. Some might feel that they should never be allowed, while others might allow a few if it is important for you to show how a particular character speaks.

In your group you might like to spend a few minutes discussing the use of swearwords. What part do they play in any language? Should you use them in your writing? How should they appear on the page if you do use them? Should we have printed them in this book?

You do not always need swearwords to be deeply insulting to someone. Consider the following incident which took place in a southern state of the USA. A white policeman has stopped a middle-aged, black driver and ordered him out of the car.

POLICEMAN: Put your hands on the car roof and stand still.
               (*He searches him.*)
               What's your name, boy?

In the southern states of America the word 'boy' is used as a condescending and insulting way for a white man to address a black man. Taken by itself the word 'boy' is not an obvious racist insult and there are many other words that we would more easily recognise as terms of racial abuse, but in this particular context 'boy' is clearly recognised as an insult by both parties.

In your group spend a few minutes identifying ways in which people speak to you that you find insulting, even though they may not use any obviously abusive words.

There are many insults that relate to a person's gender, but why is it that they are so one-sided? There are many more insulting or condescending terms for women than there are for men. Why is it that boys talk approvingly of one of their friends who goes out with a lot of girls but use an abusive word for a girl who does the same?

Where male and female versions of a word exist they are not always exact equivalents. The female version of *bachelor* is *spinster*, but the *connotations* (meanings associated with the words) are very different.

In your group discuss the meanings that you associate with *bachelor* and *spinster*. You could do the same with *master* and *mistress* and *governor* and *governess*. Can you think of any other examples like this?

Qualities that are valued in men are not always seen in the same light if demonstrated by a woman.

HE'S AMBITIOUS	**SHE'S PUSHY**
HE'S A GOOD FAMILY MAN	**SHE'S ALWAYS TAKING TIME OFF FOR THE KIDS**
HE GETS ON WELL WITH PEOPLE AT WORK	**SHE'S ALWAYS GOSSIPING**

In your group try changing the hes and shes in these two lists around and discuss the results. You may find that some of them do not sound right although they make perfectly good sense. Why is this?

Recently there has been a move to find alternatives to words that are associated with one particular gender, but there are many problems. *Headteacher* is an alternative to *headmaster* or *headmistress* but what would be the equivalent for *fireman* or *milkman*? In some cases one of the forms falls into disuse. An example of this is *poetess*, which is rarely used today. In other cases the word itself is neutral but has strong associations with one gender. An example of this is *nurse*.

In your group try to find some acceptable alternatives for the following:
manpower mankind postman master copy man-made

There are, of course, ways of being offensive without using words at all and every culture has gestures that signify contempt, ranging from signs with the fingers to sucking the teeth. In Shakespeare's time, biting your thumb at someone was regarded as an obscene gesture.

GREGORY   I will frown as I pass by, and let them take it as they list.

SAMPSON   Nay, as they dare. I will bite my thumb at them, which is a disgrace to them if they bear it.

ABRAHAM   Do you bite your thumb at us, sir?

SAMPSON   I do bite my thumb, sir.

ABRAHAM   Do you bite your thumb at us, sir?

SAMPSON   (aside to GREGORY) Is the law of our side if I say ay?

GREGORY   (aside to SAMPSON) No.

SAMPSON   No, sir, I do not bite my thumb at you, sir, but I bite my thumb, sir.

(*Romeo and Juliet*, Act I, Scene I)

As well as some words being considered unacceptable or taboo, there are also taboo subjects that people are reluctant to discuss. Sex, religion and death are topics that have been regarded as taboo in the past and still are in many societies. Sometimes the young and old have different attitudes towards their subjects.

> In your group spend a few minutes identifying any topics that you find it difficult to talk about:
>
>   a) with your friends
>   b) with older people.
>
> Are there subjects that older people seem unwilling to discuss with you?

One way of avoiding speaking directly about a sensitive subject without giving offence is to use a substitute word or **euphemism**. This is why some people might refer to a person who has died as having 'passed away' or, more **colloquially** (informal speech), 'snuffed it' or 'kicked the bucket'.

A good example of the use of euphemism is to be found in the well-known Monty Python parrot sketch, in which a customer returns a dead parrot to the pet shop where he bought it. At this point in the conversation the shop assistant has just said that the parrot is a Norwegian blue and is not dead but pining for the fjords.

CUSTOMER: It's not pining, it's passed on. This parrot is no more. It's ceased to be. It has expired. This parrot has gone to meet its maker. This is a late parrot. It's a stiff. Bereft of life, it rests in peace. If you hadn't nailed it to the perch it would be pushing up the daisies. It's run down the curtain and joined the choir invisible. It is an ex-parrot.

In your group choose something else for which there are a number of euphemisms and list as many as you can. If you are stuck for an idea, try making a list of all the euphemisms for being drunk.

Trying to Connect You

■ THE SPREAD OF THE ENGLISH LANGUAGE

By the end of the nineteenth century the British Empire covered a large part of the world and some form of English was spoken in all these areas:

These British colonies were 'conquered' for various reasons, but mainly for trade to sell British goods there and bring back raw materials like cotton and tea. The traders took English with them as did the missionaries with their hymns, bibles and prayer books. The colonies were ruled by force with no regard for local industry, culture or language.

India

Britain first went to India in the form of the East India Company to exchange goods like cotton and machines for luxury goods like tea, ivory, silk and spices. After several wars, Britain took over ruling India. Britons came in large numbers to make their fortunes. Since British people ran the economy, it was necessary for Indians to learn English.

China

China was not part of the British Empire but it was forced by the British to let western traders in, particularly opium traders. The Chinese resisted British opium traders until wars were fought and they were forced to submit. It was at this point that Britain was leased the part of China that was developed into Hong Kong. British soldiers protected British traders and missionaries and the English language spread still further.

West Africa and the Caribbean

The map below shows a triangle of trade which helps to explain why English is spoken in West Africa and the Caribbean.

British goods, like guns, were taken to West Africa, where they were exchanged for slaves who were packed into ships and were taken across the Atlantic Ocean to the Caribbean. Millions died from the hardships of the journey. Those who arrived were sold off at auction and put to work to produce cotton and sugar. Much of the sugar was used to produce rum, which was bought and drunk in large quantities on British Navy ships. The products of the slaves' work were brought back to England, where they made the ports of Liverpool and Bristol very rich.

South Africa

The Dutch were the first to colonise South Africa, but in the nineteenth century the British took over. The black population was forced to learn both languages to get work in white controlled farms and factories.

Australia and New Zealand

Australia and New Zealand were mainly settled by people from the British Isles. Some went voluntarily, others as convicts. The local people (Aborigines in Australia and Maoris in New Zealand) were forced to accept British rule and so English soon became the official language of both these countries.

Canada

In the eighteenth century there were more French than English speakers in Canada. When Britain captured the colony French settlers were forced out. French is still widely spoken in Canada now but the majority of Canadians speak English. Many Canadians are bilingual.

So the English language was taken around the world by the British in the nineteenth century and it has been strengthened and spread further in the twentieth century, through American involvement in World War Two, business, commerce, the cinema and television.

■ BRITAIN TODAY

This history of the British Empire partly explains why there are so many languages spoken in Britain today. However, it is very difficult to guess who speaks what.

> Four of these people do not speak English at home. Discuss with your group which ones you think they are.

a   b   c

d   e   f

g   h   i

These people do not speak English at home:

a) she speaks Dutch
c) he speaks Gujerati
d) he speaks Chinese
h) she speaks Welsh

You probably found that rather difficult. It is of course impossible to tell just by looking at someone what language they speak at home. It is also impossible to guess by looking at someone how many languages they speak altogether. In many classes in schools all over the country you will find that the teacher speaks only one language (is monolingual) whereas pupils in the class may be speakers of two languages (bilingual) or speakers of many languages (multilingual).

To illustrate this we are going to look at two real life examples.

BETHAN (**h** on the opposite page) lives in Wales. She goes to a school where Welsh is the main language spoken and the medium of instruction. Her science, maths and humanities lessons are taught in Welsh. Her family speaks Welsh. This is what she says about being bilingual:

> 'Being bilingual is good. But I do get fed up with the way that English is swamping Welsh. This is Wales, its language is Welsh. I am glad I am taught in Welsh at school. We speak Welsh at home and it would be silly if school used a different language.'

KETAN (**c** on the opposite page) can speak/write/read Gujerati, English and French. His school has all its lessons taught in English although he has chosen Gujerati and French as options. This is what he says about being multilingual:

> 'It doesn't seem funny to me. As soon as I get home it's Gujerati, but outside it's just English. When I started learning French at school it was quite easy, probably because it was language number three.'

When we talk about the linguistic achievements of Bethan and Ketan we need to take into account the fact that Bethan is white (and so people in Britain will assume she speaks English) and Ketan is Asian (and so a lot of people will assume either that he cannot speak English or that he will speak it badly). Issues of racism are involved in Ketan's case. This is what he says about language and racism:

> 'Sometimes blokes come up to us when we're speaking Gujerati and say "Don't speak in that language." They get angry and tell us to speak in proper English. We just keep on speaking Gujerati.'

This poem illustrates the confusion bilingual teenagers often experience:

> I dream in Bengali
> the language of my home
> my mother
> my father
> my heart.
> I dream in Bengali.
>
> I write in English
> the language of my country
> my school
> my friends
> my future.
> I write in English.
>
> Shahina Begum

During the filming of the television programmes that go with this book several bilingual pupils made reference to the confusion caused by the language position they find themselves in:

> 'I've been to India five times and they think I'm British, whereas my relatives over here think I'm Indian. I'm not sure what I am . . .'

'We've got English accents to our Gujerati. Our grandparents think that's really funny, they laugh.'

'We have community gatherings, and there you're expected to speak Gujerati. It'd be bad manners to speak in English.'

'Many Asian pupils can't speak two languages – just English.'

Some schools send letters home to parents in languages other than English because they know that in some families there are people who find it difficult to read English. Schools also do this to make a point about valuing home languages. Letters in Welsh and English might be sent in Wales and in Irish (Gaelic) in Northern Ireland.

In some schools, where there are large numbers of pupils with home languages other than English, a teacher who shares that language will be given timetabled time to help those pupils by being available to discuss things in the shared language. Sometimes other teachers will try to learn a bit of the language in order to help those pupils.

Many school libraries and class libraries contain books in many languages, including dual texts, where two languages are used.

In many schools it is recognised that pupils who can speak more than one language are a great asset to the school and have an advantage over pupils who can speak only one language. They have a lot of knowledge about language, as every day they switch from one language to another.

Many schools use a poster, shown on the next page, which says 'Welcome' in different languages to make all people feel at home and to show that all languages are of equal status.

In your group discuss what your school's attitude is to bilingual pupils' languages. Would you wish your school to change its attitude in any way? Make notes of your discussion.

JAPANESE ようこそ
MALTESE MER#BA
POLISH WITAJCIE
PERSIAN/FARSI خوش آمدید
YORUBA Ẹ KU ABỌ
FANTI AKWĀBA
SINGHALESE ඔබ ලැබ ඇත්තෙමු
BENGALI স্বাগতম
SPANISH BIENVENIDOS
TWI AKWĀBA
ARABIC مرحبا بك
MALAY SELAMAT DATANG
TAGALOG MABUHAY
URDU خوش آمدید
GERMAN WILLKOMMEN
PUNJABI ਜੀ ਆਇਆਂ ਨੂੰ
IBO ILỌ LÁ
TAMIL வணக்கம்
FRENCH BIENVENUS
HEBREW ברוכים הבאים
PORTUGUESE BEM-VINDOS
HINDI स्वागतम
CHINESE 歡迎你
SERBO-CROAT DOBRODOŠLI
GREEK ΚΑΛΩΣΟΡΙΣΕΤΕ
VIETNAMESE HOAN NGHÊNH
GUZARATI ભલે પધાર્યા
ENGLISH WELCOME
ITALIAN BENVENUTI
TURKISH HOŞ GELDİNİZ

■ ASSIGNMENT 2
A school language policy

By now you should have notes from the last three units from which you can plan and write an assignment.

'Talking Proper' should have helped you decide how you feel about the way you speak and how other people speak. It should have helped you to see why Standard English occupies the place it does.

'Sticks and Stones' looked at swearwords, racist and sexist language and taboo subjects.

In 'Trying to Connect You' the need to value languages other than English which are to be found in Britain largely as a result of the British Empire, was stressed.

Using these notes plan an assignment which sets out an ideal school language policy.

You could structure your assignment in the following way:

1 INTRODUCTION. Why a school language policy?
2 STANDARD ENGLISH
3 UNACCEPTABLE LANGUAGE
4 LANGUAGES OTHER THAN ENGLISH
5 CONCLUSION. How staff and pupils could put their ideas into practice.

Plan your assignment first. This could be done in discussion with your partner or your group. Then write your rough draft. Show this to as many people as possible and consider their opinions when you are redrafting for your final draft. Make sure the style you use is suitable for a school policy statement. You could look at an example of one of your school's policy statements.

PART 3: A Language Issue

WHAT BIG TEETH YOU HAVE, GRAMMAR

In this unit you will consider some of the differences between talking and writing. We describe the complexities of the writing process and invite you to consider matching purpose and audience. The unit concludes with a section on spelling.

IN YOUR HANDS

In this unit you will consider the meaning of the word 'grammar' and the terms that are associated with it. You will be asked to consider how grammar varies, how we learn it and whether it is really as difficult as people think.

PROFESSIONAL BOXERS

In this unit you will examine the use of spoken language in the media and consider the part played by gesture and facial expression. You will also consider the language styles of different programmes.

ASSIGNMENT 3

You will be asked to gather evidence from a variety of sources to show that language is still a controversial issue. A possible structure is offered to help you present your findings.

Make and keep notes on all these issues for Assignment 3

What Big Teeth You Have, Grammar

The subject of **grammar** is often in the news. There are many different views as to what grammar is and extravagant claims are made for it. One reason it is included in this book is because the laws concerned with education insist that you know about it.

Some aspects of grammar you know about already, without being taught anything. Other aspects may be new to you. The terms introduced in this unit may be useful when discussing language, but knowing them will not necessarily make you a better reader, writer or talker.

We begin with three of the many descriptions of grammar.

■ DESCRIPTIONS OF GRAMMAR

A popular view of the word grammar is that it refers to a set of fixed rules about the 'dos' and 'don'ts' of language, as in the cartoon on page 71. These rules can be found in grammar books, which date back to the eighteenth and nineteenth centuries. Very often this view takes no account of the changes in English over time, nor of the regional variety in the language.

There is another view of grammar that refers to the way grammar used to be taught in schools. This involved learning the parts of speech (noun, verb, etc.) and parsing (identifying the function of phrases and clauses in sentences). All this was closely related to the way Latin was taught. The problem is that Latin, unlike English, does not change, because it is not a 'living' language.

Another way to think of grammar is like a set of rules for playing a game, such as chess. The rules define the moves of each piece, but allow for an infinite number of different games. Unlike chess, we do not have to be taught the rules. We learn the grammar of a language as we grow up and soon invent sentences of our own. This view sees grammar as offering a framework for producing language.

As a speaker of English, you will be able to invent sentences that probably no-one has spoken or written before. This is because you already know the grammar of the language. Here is an example:

Red-tailed cows dance to jazz bands on Friday nights.

Now, you produce a sentence that you think nobody has ever used before.

■ SYNTAX

Grammar enables us to create an infinite number of sentences, spoken or written. It also provides the rules for arranging words in the right order, so that the sentences we produce are meaningful. The order of words is called **syntax**, and you will quickly notice when the word order, or syntax, is wrong. You will not need to be taught it, unless you are learning English as a foreign language.

Written like this the following words make little or no sense.

a bee twice the woman stung yesterday

Alter the word order to produce as many different grammatical sentences as you can. As you change words round, so you will change the meaning.

The word order we use for speaking and writing is usually the same. But there are other differences between the way we speak and the way we write.

Read the following extracts. One is a piece of writing. The other is a transcript of someone talking. Which is which?

'I think the Mid-West is the dullest of the American accents cos it's . . . they . . . we don't really . . . I think to some people we sound a little nasal . . . but . . . um . . . like there aren't any expressions that set us apart from other Americans.'

'I think the Mid-West is the dullest of the American accents. I think, to some people, we sound a little nasal. Also, there aren't any expressions that set us apart from other Americans.'

One key difference is that we write but do not talk in sentences, unless the talk is of a formal nature. Most grammars place considerable emphasis on the sentence as the basis for studying language. But what is a sentence?

Here are three definitions of a sentence:

1 A group of words that start with a capital letter and end with a full stop (child's definition)
2 A number of words that make sense (adult's definition)
3 The complete expression of a single thought (dictionary definition)

Now ask your teachers, parents and friends for a definition. Consult dictionaries. Write down all the answers you get and then compare them. Have you found a satisfactory definition of a sentence?

■ MORPHOLOGY

Syntax is about the order in which we put words together. **Morphology** is about the way we change parts of the words themselves.

For example, in the sentence:

The girl looks happy

we can make changes to individual words. Thus:

girl can become girls (singular to plural)
looks can become looked (present to past tense)
happy can become unhappy (adding the prefix 'un')

So we can produce the sentence:

The girls looked unhappy

Learning the different ways that words can change is not easy. Young children often make mistakes and so do adults. The more experience we have of language, the fewer mistakes we make.

In order that you understand what morphology means, see what changes you can make to the following words:

Change these from singular to plural: **box tooth mouse.**
Change these from present to past: **smile run write.**
Alter these by adding a prefix: **certain obey legible.**

Then alter these words by adding an appropriate suffix. You may need to alter the spelling: **sad beauty merry**

Nouns alter according to whether they are singular or plural. But notice that some singular nouns refer to several items, e.g. baggage.
    Some plural nouns refer to singular items, e.g. trousers.

Can you think of similar examples?

Verbs alter according to whether the time is past, present or future. But notice the exception with newspaper headlines like 'GIRL ESCAPES DEATH' or 'WELSH TEAM WINS', which refer to past events.

Can you find other examples like this?

Verbs also alter according to mood, according to whether they are active or passive. To illustrate this we can look at an incident from the Second World War.
    General Eisenhower wrote a press statement that said: 'The troops have been withdrawn' (passive). He recognised that by expressing the decision this way he was avoiding his own responsibilities, so he rewrote it: 'I have withdrawn the troops' (active).

In your group, decide how to rewrite these statements in the active voice:

A decision has been taken.   **Trespassers will be prosecuted.**
It has come to my notice.   **The culprits have been warned.**

So, syntax and morphology are the key elements of grammar.

■ PARTS OF SPEECH

Some people mistakenly think that knowing the parts of speech is the same as knowing grammar. Sometimes it may be useful to be familiar with this particular classification of words, if you are discussing a piece of writing, for example. This knowledge will not, however, make you a better writer.

Traditionally, there are eight classes of word:

nouns	e.g.	dog, pencil, truth
pronouns	e.g.	she, her, it
adjectives	e.g.	grey, short, neat
verbs	e.g.	bark, write, think
adverbs	e.g.	loudly, neatly, often
prepositions	e.g.	in, for, under
conjunctions	e.g.	and, but, because
interjections	e.g.	ouch! help!

Each of these word classes has a different function. In a sentence you can interchange only words of the same type. So a noun can replace a noun; a verb can replace a verb, and so on. Using this knowledge, which you will have acquired yourself, and the rules of syntax, you can create an infinite number of sentences. For example:

Dogs   **bark**   **loudly.**
(noun)   (verb)   (adverb)

In place of 'dogs', you could write 'wolves' or another noun.
In place of 'bark', you could write 'howl' or another verb.
In place of 'loudly', you could write 'often' or another adverb.

Defining precisely what all these terms mean may prove quite difficult. Common definitions can be quite unhelpful.

In your group discuss the following poem and whether or not it is
useful to know what the parts of speech are.

Poem

The teacher said:
A noun is a naming word.
What is a naming word
in the sentence
'He named the ship, Lusitania'?
'Named' said George.
'WRONG – it's ship.'

The teacher said:
A verb is a doing word.
What is the doing word
in the sentence
'I like doing homework'?
'Doing' said George.
'WRONG – it's like.'

The teacher said:
An adjective is a describing word.
What is the describing word
in the sentence
'Describing sunsets is boring'?
'Describing' said George.
'WRONG – it's boring.'
'I know it is,' said George.

Mike Rosen

There are some words that belong to more than one class. Their meaning
depends on the rest of the sentence. The word *round*, for example, can be a
noun, a verb, an adjective, an adverb and a preposition.

In your group, try to produce five sentences to show how this can be.

■ CHANGES OVER TIME

One of the problems with some definitions of grammar is the failure to recognise that English grammar has changed over the years.

If you read a passage of English, written many years ago, you will notice at once different words, different spellings, and if you go back a thousand years or so, different letters.

> Read the four extracts from the Bible (1 Corinthians 13). In your group complete the chart over the page by recording some of the changes that have taken place. Notice also the many similarities between the passages.

Whanne I was a litil child, I spak as a litil child, I undurstood as a litil child, I thoughte as a litil child; but whanne I was maad a man, I avoided tho thingis that weren of a litil child. And we seen now bi a myrour in derknesse, but thanne face to face; now I knowe of parti, but than I schal knowe, as I am knowen.

c. 1395

When I was a chylde, I spake as a chylde, I understode as a chylde, I ymagened as a chylde. But assone as I was a man, I put away chyldeshnes. Now we se in a glasse, even in a darke speakynge: but then shall we se face to face. Now I knowe unparfectly: but then shall I knowe even as I am knowen.

1535

When I was a child, I spake as a child, I understood as a child, I thought as a child: but when I became a man, I put away childish things. For now we see through a glass, darkly; but then face to face: now I know in part; but then shall I know even as I am known.

1611 (in edition of 1873)

When I was a child, my speech, my outlook, and my thoughts were all childish. When I grew up, I had finished with childish things. Now we see only puzzling reflections in a mirror, but then we shall see face to face. My knowledge now is partial; then it will be whole, like God's knowledge of me.

1961

c. 1395	1535	1611	1961
spak		spake	—
		understood	—
	—		things
		see	
of parti			—
	knowen		—

■ ASSESSING WRITING

We learn grammar young. We learn it as we use language in everyday life and long before we go to school. Here is some writing from five-year-old Alexis. The spelling is certainly confused and the writing could easily be dismissed as hopelessly ungrammatical, but look at its positive qualities:

correct word order
correct use of present and past tense
a style and tone suitable for its purpose
the effective use of repetition for emphasis . . .

to Daddy
I am sorry
but I did want a
balloon I am
sorry that I cried
I am sorry Daddy

Now write an assessment of this writing for the parents of the child. Say how far you think the writing is clear, accurate, appropriate and effective. Is there anything ungrammatical?

Now you should know a little more about what grammar is and is not.

Use your responses to this unit of work, and to the television programme, if you watched it, to explain what 'grammar' means . . . and what it does not.
   This could be in the form of a poem, like that of Mike Rosen.

See page 100 for the assignment that relates to this unit.

In Your Hands

■ WHY WRITE?

Here are some school students' answers to that question:

it will help me to get a job

because I have to

to pass exams

I like it

my teacher makes me

I enjoy writing

everyone writes

Most people would agree that one important reason for writing is to communicate with other people. However, this is also true of speaking. It is interesting to look at ways in which writing helps us to communicate in ways we cannot simply by speaking. By writing we can:

- make our thoughts and ideas available to many people, e.g. books
- keep our thoughts and ideas, e.g. diaries
- send our thoughts and ideas to other people who live a long way away from us, e.g. letters
- plan what we want to say in more detail, e.g. notes for an essay
- show our first ideas to other people and alter what we want to say according to their opinions, e.g. redrafting
- present our thoughts and ideas in a highly finished state, e.g. assignments
- demonstrate our knowledge to other people, e.g. written exams
- keep a record of what people say or what we read, e.g. revision notes

Discuss which of the above purposes you use writing for. Can you add more to the list? Which do you think is the most important?

■ THE DIFFERENCES BETWEEN TALKING AND WRITING

Now we will think about the differences between talking and writing. Each of us hears and uses talk all the time but we do not often see it written down. What follows is a transcript from the filming for the television programmes that go with this book, and is an excellent example of collaborative talk. Four students are discussing a job survey that will go in their school newspaper:

We've only got a week to do this in and we're going to probably have to stay after school.

Yeah, and we're probably going to have to do it in a way everyone can sort of answer quickly.

I think we should do a survey and then everyone . . .

Yeah, that would be good we could type it up, if we type it up on the computer we could get it out quickly.

I mean there would have to be sort of, I mean it won't have to be very long.

(all talking) answer very quickly and not like big questions, (all talking) and if we get some interesting ones we can do some interviews or whatever . . .

Yeah, so interview a few of the people who (all talking) work 15 hours a day.

Do you think we're going to get many because (all talking)

We send it out the first year's not likely to have many jobs.

Fifth year . . .

But the fourth and fifth year.

The fifth year's doing exams now so we can't send out . . .

And the fourth year's going on work experience . . .

But I mean . . .

. . . quite a lot of answers.

Yeah.

We need a way to get all the answers in quickly from all the school.

Go around at registration take too long.

Yes, yes.

We could to a survey because in that way we could get everyone's answers.

Yes. If we sent it out in the registers that would be good.

It can't be too long, and the questions have got to be short.

And we need precise answers as well, maybe interview someone or . . .

Yes, anyone who has a really interesting job.

If we get answers which are like really, you know people working long (15 hours a week or whatever).

Working in small groups, note down all the things that seem strange about the above extract when considered just as a piece of writing. Remember that it is a transcript of a conversation.

Here is another example of talk written down. This is from the same transcript and is part of an interview for the job survey. The student has been asked the question 'How did you get the job?'

'Well, I goes to my cousin, Alex and I says to him, Alex, I need a job and he says OK then he goes away and 2 week, 2 days later he comes back to me and says, OK then, I've got a job for you, yeah, there's a butcher's and I goes OK but how much will I be earning, and he goes £20 and I goes, all right then, not bad.'

Think about how this would have been written if it had been a piece of writing rather than a piece of talk. What would be the main thing you would have to change if you wrote it out?

From the work you have done above you should have found out for yourself that the main differences between talking and writing are:

- talk is something you do with other people; writing is usually something you do on your own (although you need other people to help you on the way as the television programme that corresponds with this unit demonstrates)

- talk goes, unless people remember it; writing stays on the page

- talk is unfinished, repetitive and usually dependent on facial expressions, gestures and tone of voice for its meaning; writing is often highly finished (although it need not be) and dependent on punctuation, grammar and syntax for its meaning.

■ THE WRITING PROCESS

When we write something we often have to do many complicated things:

- we have an idea for something to write, or we are told to write something and we then have an idea about it

- we make sure we are clear about what we are doing, who is the audience, how much time we have to complete the task

- we often talk to someone about it

- we write a rough draft (to do this we need to be able to pick up a pen and use it correctly or know how to use a keyboard)

- we show it to other people

- we redraft it

- we decide what the finished product will look like

- we write the final draft

- we deal with responses to what we have written, as writing is for an audience (which might be just you) and readers always have opinions about what they have read.

This is what happened when one of us started writing this unit:

'We had lots of discussions about what would go in a unit called In Your Hands but I knew I had to begin the actual writing. I did not want to do it very much, even though I had kept a morning to get started on it. After lots of delaying tactics, like eating toast as well as cereal for breakfast and doing some background reading on the subject, I decided to have a bath and think through in detail what would go into the unit. Next I drew out a skeleton plan of what would go in. It looked like this:

why → write?: Difference between talking and writing
Writing process — ideas
　　　　　　　　 - plan
　　　　　　　　 - talk
NB physical skill ↗ 　 - rough draft / re draft
　　　　　　　　 - audience
　　　　　　　　 - presentation
　　　　　 ✳ -responses ✳

Pupils' own writing - why?
　　　　　　　　　 - what?
　　　　　　　　　 -for whom?

Spelling - matters in writing / not talking
　　　　　　 also punctuation

appropriateness

'I reminded myself of my audience and considered whether I had covered all the things they would need to think about. Having done that I realised I had missed out some important things. I added them to my plan.

'I arranged to meet one of the other authors to discuss my first ideas. We talked about what I had planned and made some changes after our discussion.

'That evening I went back to my word-processor and started to write out the unit in full.'

Look back at the list of things we do when we write and you will see that the writer did many of the things at the beginning of the list. Now try it for yourself with a very short assignment.

Imagine that the best teacher you have ever had is about to leave the school. Someone comes round with a card for you to sign. Even though it is a bit embarrassing you want to let that teacher know how good you think s/he is and how much you will miss her/him. Plan the message that you will write and then write it exactly as you would in the card.

Although this bit of writing is very short you should still have done a lot of the things on the list on page 86. You will have planned, considered the purpose and audience for the writing, you may well have discussed what you were doing with someone else, you may have written it in rough first and you will certainly have made sure that the words you used said what you wanted to say. You probably also checked your spelling, punctuation and handwriting. So writing is not simply a question of picking up a pen and making some marks on paper.

■ THE RANGE OF WRITING

Make a chart, like the one that has been started below, to show all the different kinds of writing that you do, why you do them and who you do them for.

WHAT	WHY	AUDIENCE
essays	part of my exam	teachers
letters		friends
	need more milk	

Your chart probably shows you that you do a wide range of writing for a variety of purposes and a variety of audiences. You also change the way you write to suit the purpose and audience. Consider this note to a milkman:

10, Rose Walk,
Trupton,
Wessex.
HO2 2UB

8 April 1990

The Milk Float,
Somewhere Down the Road,
Trupton,
Wessex.
HO2 2UB

Dear Sir,

I would be most grateful if you would be kind enough to leave one extra pint of milk today.

I trust that you and your family are in good health and that you enjoyed your recent holiday.

Yours faithfully,

C. Yeobright (Mr)

Discuss why this is a strange note to leave for a milkman. Consider whether it is appropriate in terms of its purpose, topic and audience.

Pick one of the other kinds of writing from your chart and write inappropriately for your purpose, topic and audience, e.g. you could write a letter to a friend like a formal report, or the beginning of an examination in a chatty, informal style. Remember to make the vocabulary inappropriate as well as the style and tone.

■ SPELLING

When you get to a final draft one of the things you look at is spelling. Some people seem to think that spelling is the most important aspect of writing. It is not, content is far more important. However, it is important to spell words in the same way as other people in order to make sure your meaning is clear.

If you think of spelling as a sport, then a dictionary is a description of the state of play, not the rules of the game. It tells you how words are spelt now but this does not mean that they were always spelt this way or will be spelt this way in the future. Until the eighteenth century people used to write down words very much as they heard them and there are examples of many different ways of spelling the same word. This was also true of people's names and there are examples of Shakespeare's name being spelt *Shakespear* and *Shakespere*.

When some people tried to standardise spelling it was often a matter of chance which spelling of a word they chose. It was not always the most common one and often more than one version continued to be used. A good example of this is *gaol* and *jail*. They both appear in the dictionary although *gaol* is not used very often today.

Sometimes there is more than one version of a word because it is spelt differently in another dialect of English, e.g. in American English *colour* is spelt *color*.

In your group, try to find some other words that are spelt in more than one way. Discuss why this might be so.

How do we learn to spell? We might start by trying to write words as they sound but we find out very quickly that this does not work very often. Because English words have developed from a number of different languages the same group of letters can often represent a number of different sounds. A good example of this is -ough, which can be pronounced in at least seven different ways, depending on the word in which it is used, e.g. cough, bough, dough, hiccough, thorough, through, tough.

George Bernard Shaw once suggested that *fish* could be spelt *ghoti*. When asked what he meant he explained as follows:

gh as in cough

o   as in women

ti as in nation

Another way is to learn spelling rules such as *i before e except after c*. Some of these, such as this example, are quite useful but most of them have so many exceptions that they may only confuse you. In an experiment a computer was programmed with 300 spelling rules but was still only able to spell correctly less than half of the words in the sample.

Some people have suggested that all you need to do is encourage people to read and they will automatically learn how to spell. Unfortunately, this does not really work because when we read our eyes do not stop on each individual word, we scan whole chunks at a time, which is why we are sometimes fooled by tricks such as:

**TOP OF THE
THE POPS**

There is no simple answer to the question *How do we learn to spell?* but there are some things that we do know.

If we invent a word **KNOTTLE**, say it to people and ask them to write it down they will probably start by spelling it the way it sounds. They might spell it the way that we intended but they might also spell it:

NOTTLE   NOTTEL   or   KNOTTEL

If we then tell them that a **KNOTTLE** is a device for untangling string, they might guess that it belongs to the family of words that are built around **KNOT** and probably has a silent **K**. This will leave them with

KNOTTLE   or   KNOTTEL

However, they will probably realise that *-OTTEL* is an unusual grouping of letters in English and that *-OTTLE* as in **BOTTLE** and **THROTTLE** is much more common. They will probably conclude that **KNOTTLE** is the most likely spelling.

So, some of the ways that we arrive at spellings are by considering:

- What the word sounds like
- What the word means
- Which family of words it is likely to belong to
- Which combinations of letters are most common in English

See page 100 for the assignment that relates to this unit.

Professional Boxers

When you watch people talking on the television it is not just what they are saying that conveys meaning. We receive additional information from the person's body language, their gestures and their facial expression. Try turning off the picture, using the brightness control, and then listen to one of the TV 'soaps'. How easy is it to tell what is going on?

Now try watching the picture with the sound turned down. How much of the plot can you understand just from the gestures and facial expressions?

If you compare a TV 'soap' with one on the radio, such as *The Archers* or *Citizens* (Radio 4), you will notice differences in the way that people speak. You cannot see gestures and expressions on the radio and so these must be conveyed by the *way* in which people speak. They may vary their speed, volume, tone and the stress they place on particular words to convey their feelings.

> In your groups try saying this sentence in three different ways to express the following moods: **a) angry b) pleading c) frustrated**
> 'You can't leave it there, it's blocking up the entire road.'

You can express a wide range of feelings by the way you say an individual word.

> Try saying 'hamburger' to express the following:
>
> **a) puzzlement b) surprise c) delight d) disgust**

We expect particular styles of presentation on particular programmes. We do not expect the news to be read in the style of a stand-up comic and we all see the joke when there is a deliberate mismatch between the style and content of a programme.

Here is a Saturday morning trip to the supermarket described in the style of (a) a sports programme and (b) a traffic report.

a) 'And there's a hush settling on the crowd here at the city shopping centre as we wait for the doors to open for the Saturday supermarket stakes. We have a field of about thirty – not the biggest we've seen, Peter?'

'No, indeed, Ron. Back in 1987 we had a field of thirty-five – all the more surprising because the aisles were still only five feet wide. They have, of course, since been widened to bring us up to the European standard of two metres.'

'But, of course, that was before the introduction of the wider trolley.'

'Yes, but the older style, narrow ones are still available and this is one of the crucial decisions that competitors have to make. Do they go for greater capacity or manoeuvrability?'

'Wait a minute – yes – they're off, and there's no clear leader yet as they break for the trolleys. And it's over to Derek in the cigarette kiosk . . .'

b) 'And there's a ten-yard tailback on aisle 3 where a trolley has shed its load near the frozen foods. Anyone heading for wines and spirits is advised to take a diversion via home baking ingredients. Traffic is building up at all checkouts but shoppers who are able to pay by cash could save themselves time by using checkout 9. There are long delays at checkout 7, where the assistant is trying to get someone to find out the price of kumquats, and checkout 2 has been coned off due to the spillage of a large jar of pickled onions.'

This deliberate mimicking of a style is called **parody**. Try describing your journey to school in the style of a) or b) or of one of the following: **c) a police report d) a game show**

You will rarely hear anyone on TV speak in a dialect other than Standard English, except in films or plays, or perhaps someone being interviewed for a documentary programme or news item. You will usually hear people speaking Standard English with a regional accent but some regional accents seem to be more acceptable than others for nationally broadcast programmes.

In your group discuss which of the following people's accents you think would not be acceptable for the national evening news and why?

   a) **Derek Jameson**   b) **Cilla Black**   c) **Terry Wogan**
   d) **Floella Benjamin** e) **Billy Connolly**   f) **Clive James**

HERE IS THE NEWS

Most of the language that people use on television is, in fact, written language. They may be saying it but in the case of newsreaders and announcers they are reading it from a teleprompt and in drama series they have learned their lines from written scripts.

It is very difficult to make people sound natural when they are using scripted words. 'Just a Minute' is a radio programme in which celebrities try to speak for one minute on a given topic without hesitating, repeating themselves, or straying from the subject matter. This is very difficult because in everyday speech we constantly hesitate, repeat ourselves and stray from the point.

In your group take it in turns to speak about a subject that someone else chooses for you without hesitating, repeating yourself, or straying from the subject matter. If you find this too difficult, try choosing your own subject. Does this make any difference?

In everyday speech we rarely speak in complete sentences, we interrupt one another, speak at the same time and leave things out if the other person already knows them. On television it is difficult to have more than one person speaking at a time and you must let the audience in on what the characters know.

Over the page is an extract from the script of an episode of a comedy series called *Houseful*, which is about a couple, Jack and Lynn Kennedy, who have two children of their own, Tom and Julie, but also foster six other children. They live in a big, old Victorian house in Bournemouth and in this scene it is breakfast time.

How like everyday speech is it? You might notice that although there are a large number of people in the kitchen there only seems to be one conversation going on at a time. Is this realistic?

1 The kitchen

Jack is at the cooker putting out the flames in the grill pan. Lynn is reading a newspaper. Four of the younger children are sitting around the huge kitchen table eating toast and cereal. Tom enters and slams the door.

JACK	Do you think you could leave the hinges on next time, Tom?
TOM	Do I detect the aroma of char-grilled sausages again, with the accent on char? Shall I go and take the battery out of the smoke detector before it goes off for the third time this week?
JACK	If you've got any complaints you're quite welcome to make your own breakfast.
TOM	Thanks for the offer, Dad, but I've got to go. I've got other fish to fry, not to mention sausages to burn.

Tom leaves, slamming the door on his way out.

TOM	I swear I heard some more tiles fall off the roof.
LYNN	Well, I don't think you should put in another insurance claim.
TOM	Why not? Storm damage is a perfectly valid reason for claiming.
LYNN	But the hurricane was years ago.
TOM	Yes, but it's a delayed reaction. Hurricanes just set off a chain of destruction.
LYNN	Pretty long chain.

A squabble has broken out at one end of the table.

SALLY	It's not fair.
TRACY	'Tis.
SALLY	'Tisn't.
LYNN	What is?
SALLY	Isn't.
TRACY	Is.
SALLY	Isn't.
LYNN	Enough! Now, what's all this about?
SALLY	She took the megadeath blaster from the Krispy Krunch packet

and it was my turn, 'cos she had the astrospinner from the Wheatipuffs last week.

TRACY   Yeah? And what about the pop pinup cards from the Sugar Snaps and the scratch 'n' sniff diesel juggernaut from the Fibreflakes?

TOM   Whatever happened to good old gruel?

Gary and Sharon arrive at the same time, jostling and shoving each other.

LYNN   What's taken you two so long?

GARY   Ask her, I thought she'd moved into the bathroom permanently. I had to wait ages to take a shower.

SHARON   Sorry, I didn't realise it was your birthday.

GARY   It isn't . . . oh, very funny. At least I don't have to disguise myself with half an inch of putty before I go out.

SHARON   No, but it might be kinder if you did.

GARY   We're not all obsessed with our bodies, you know.

SHARON   No? What's this, then?

She reaches into a cupboard and produces a set of chest expanders. Gary looks embarrassed.

SHARON   No, no, let me guess. A hammock for the cat? A catapult for launching skateboarders? A spare part for your granny's corset?

GARY   At least I can develop my body, yours is more in need of demolition. Do you know what Kenny Procter said about you on the way home yesterday?

SHARON   What?

GARY   He said, 'I can tell that Sharon lives around here.' I said, 'Why?' He said, 'Dents in the pavement.'

Sharon starts to chase Gary round the table, brandishing the chest expanders.

If you are able to, make a recording of a group of friends chatting. Try transcribing a short section exactly as it took place and then compare it with the extract from *Houseful*. What are the main differences that you notice?

■ ASSIGNMENT 3
A language issue

At the beginning of this book we pointed out that language is still a controversial subject. In the last three units we examined some of these issues in more detail. In 'What Big Teeth You Have, Grammar', we looked at what grammar is, as opposed to what many people think it is. 'In Your Hands' looked at the process of writing, including the always popular topic of spelling, and 'Professional Boxers' examined some of the language styles to be encountered in television and radio.

As well as news stories that appear from time to time, you will probably have seen advertisements that play on people's insecurities about their language by asking:

Why Are You Shamed By Your Mistakes In English?

A SIMPLE technique for acquiring a swift mastery of good English has just been announced. It can double your powers of self-expression. It can pay you real dividends in business and social advancement, and give you added poise, self-confidence, and personal effectiveness.

Many people do not realise how much they could influence others simply by speaking and writing with greater power, authority, and precision. Whether you are presenting a report, training a child, fighting for a cause, making a sale, writing an essay, or asking for a rise . . . your success depends

There are also, from time to time, letters from people complaining about the way in which an article has been written or the way that a newsreader has read an item on the radio or television.

Some of the views expressed show that these people are what we might call linguistic 'flat earthers'*. By this we mean that in order to hold these views you have to ignore everything that we have learnt about language in the past 100 years. This is just like still believing that the Earth is flat, despite all the evidence to the contrary. You should now be ready to write an assignment about the ways in which language is still a burning issue.

* *In* Language, Ignorance and Education *by Geoffrey Thornton.*

- To prepare for this assignment you should collect evidence in the form of as many articles, advertisements and letters about language as you can from recent newspapers and magazines. For examples, look back to the opening page of 'Whose English?' You could also gather information from the television series that accompanies this book and ask people you know for their views.

- Sort your evidence into different categories. Is it concerned with talk, reading or writing? Is it about accent, dialect, grammar, spelling etc.? Does it demonstrate any real knowledge or merely reveal someone's prejudices? Discuss these points with someone else.

- You should now be ready to plan your first draft. Your plan might look something like this:

① My evidence → Where I found it
→ what it was about

② Do I agree with what is being said?

③ Does any of it concern me?

④ How I feel about my own languages.

- You should now write your first draft. Discuss it with other people and make any changes that you think are necessary before you write your final version.

PART 4: The Heart of the Language

This part contains four extracts from:

Talking Heads by Alan Bennett (a dramatic monologue from television)

Romeo and Juliet by William Shakespeare (1564–1616) (a play)

'Still I Rise' by Maya Angelou (a poem)

Pride and Prejudice by Jane Austen (1775–1817) (a novel)

We have taken the title of this part very literally. All four extracts deal with affairs of the heart. The Shakespeare, Bennett and Austen extracts deal with the relationships between young men and young women. The Maya Angelou poem is about the relationship between the writer and the reader.

Several short activities are suggested for each extract. Our focus is on the way language has been used to achieve the writer's purpose and to create a unique piece of literature. You may wish to develop one of our activities into a substantial assignment in the style of one of the extracts.

We end the book with poems written by school students, for you to read and enjoy. Our follow-up assignment is for you to use the ideas in the book to create a piece of literature through the powerful use of your own language. We have left a symbolic space for you at the end.

■ TALKING HEADS

This passage is an extract from a television play by Alan Bennett. Lesley is telling us about what happened to her when she met Spud.

Now my hobby is people.
I collect people.
So when I saw this interesting-looking man in the corner, next thing is – I find myself talking to him. I said: 'You look an interesting person. I'm interested in interesting people. Hello.'
He said: 'Hello.'
I said: 'What do you do?'
He said: 'I'm in films.'
I said: 'Oh, that's interesting, anything in the pipeline?'
He said: 'As a matter of fact, yes –'
and starts telling me about this project he's involved in, making videos for the overseas market, targeted chiefly on West Germany.
I said: 'Are you the producer?'
He said: 'No – but I'm on the production side, the name's Spud.'
I said: 'Spud. That's an interesting name, mine's Lesley.'
He said: 'As it happens, Lesley, we've got a problem at the moment. Our main girl has had to drop out because her back's packed in, are you an actress?'
I said: 'Well, Spud, it's interesting you should ask, because as a matter of fact I am.'
He said: 'Will you excuse me one moment, Lesley.'
I said: 'Why, Spud, where are you going?'
He said: 'I'm going to go away, Lesley, and make one phone call.'

It transpires the director is seeing possible replacements the very next day, at an address in West London.
Spud said: 'It's interesting, because I'm based in Ealing.'
I said: 'Isn't that West London?'
He said: 'It is. Where's your stamping ground?'

►

I said: 'Bromley, for my sins.'

He said: 'That's far-ish away. Why not bed down at my place?'

I said: 'Thank you, kind sir, but I didn't fall off the Christmas tree yesterday.'

He said: 'Lesley, I've got a son studying hotel management and a daughter with one kidney. Besides, I've got my sister-in-law staying. She's come up for the Ideal Home Exhibition.'

The penny began to drop when I saw the tattoo. My experience of tattoos is that they're generally confined to the lower echelons, and when I saw his vest – it had electrician written all over it. I never even saw the sister-in-law. Still traipsing round Olympia, probably . . .

In your group, note all the information in the passage about Lesley, Spud and the situation. How much of this information do you think is true?

Although Lesley is telling the story, we are not really very sympathetic towards her. Why is this?

In your groups, discuss which of the following statements about Lesley you agree or disagree with:

- We laugh at Lesley because she keeps saying 'interesting'.
- Lesley is stupid because she does not recognise all the clues which show that Spud is not offering her a decent job.
- Lesley tries to be clever but uses too many clichés.
- Lesley is a snob.
- Lesley's language is very simple, especially when talking to Spud.

The extract is amusing because of the characters involved and the situation itself. Much of the humour is based on irony because both we and the author are laughing at the character, despite her serious intentions. In the opening lines, for example, Lesley says, 'I collect people', as if she were a powerful person. In fact, Spud collects her. She also identifies Spud as an interesting person, which he clearly is not.

> In your groups, find other examples of humour in the passage and discuss why you find them funny.

The layout of this passage is like a play, with the *He said/I said* pattern being repeated like a script. This turns the passage into a play within a play, although, in fact, it is really a monologue.

> In your group, discuss how effective you think this style and format are as a means of exploring the character of Lesley.

■ ROMEO AND JULIET

In the following passage from Shakespeare's *Romeo and Juliet*, Romeo has secretly entered Juliet's room and has spent the night with her. It is now dawn and Romeo must leave before he is discovered.

JULIET: Wilt thou be gone? it is not yet near day:
           It was the nightingale, and not the lark,
           That pierc'd the fearful hollow of thine ear;
           Nightly she sings on yon pomegranate tree:
           Believe me, love, it was the nightingale.
ROMEO: It was the lark, the herald of the morn,
           No nightingale: look, love, what envious streaks
           Do lace the severing clouds in yonder east:
           Night's candles are burnt out, and jocund day
           Stands tiptoe on the misty mountain tops.
           I must be gone and live, or stay and die.

▶

JULIET: Yon light is not daylight, I know it, I:
It is some meteor that the sun exhales,
To be to thee this night a torch-bearer,
And light thee on thy way to Mantua:
Therefore stay yet, thou need'st not to be gone.

ROMEO: Let me be ta'en, let me be put to death;
I am content, so thou wilt have it so.
I'll say yon gray is not the morning's eye,
'Tis but the pale reflex of Cynthia's brow;
Nor that is not the lark whose notes do beat
The vaulty heaven so high above our heads:
I have more care to stay than will to go.
Come, death, and welcome, Juliet wills it so.
How is't, my soul? Let's talk; it is not day.

JULIET: It is, it is, hie hence, be gone, away!
It is the lark that sings so out of tune,
Straining harsh discords and unpleasing sharps.
Some say the lark makes sweet division;
This doth not so, for she divideth us:
Some say the lark and loathed toad change eyes;
O, now I would they had chang'd voices too!
Since arm from arm that voice doth us affray,
Hunting thee hence with hunt's-up to the day.
O, now be gone; more light and light it grows!

ROMEO: More light and light, more dark and dark our woes!

    Act III, Scene V

When you read a text that was written hundreds of years ago, there may well be words with which you are unfamiliar and situations that you do not fully understand.

Make a list of questions that you would need to ask in order to fully understand this passage. Compare your list with those of others in your group; some of you may have information that you can share with the others.

Although this is an excerpt from a play, the language is poetic and Shakespeare uses many literary devices to give it its richness. These include:

Alliteration: The repetition of consonant sounds.

'Hunting thee hence with hunt's-up to the day.'

Assonance: The repetition of vowel sounds.

'loathed toad.'

Personification: Giving a human character to inanimate objects or abstract ideas.

'. . . and jocund day
Stands tiptoe on the misty mountain tops.'

You will be able to find many other examples of these figures of speech. Another device used throughout this passage is that of opposition, e.g. light/dark.

In your group make a list of all the words and phrases associated with sound. Next, divide your list into pleasant and unpleasant sounds, e.g.:

Pleasant	**Unpleasant**
notes	harsh discords

Why do you think that there are so many examples of opposites in the language of this play?

The play takes place within a divided community, caused, in this case, by a family feud. If this scene were to take place now, in a divided community such as Belfast or Beirut, images such as the lark and nightingale might seem inappropriate.

In your group, discuss the sorts of images that you might wish to use if you were to re-write this scene in a modern setting.

■ STILL I RISE

Read the poem by Maya Angelou first and then read the notes around it, which raise ideas about what is said and how it has been written.

Who is 'me'?
this is a way of working out rhyme sche[me]

Who is 'you'?

You may write me down in history A
With your bitter, twisted lies, B
You may trod me in the very dirt C
But still, like dust, I'll rise. B

like dust

trod?

I'll rise (in the futur[e])

Sassiness?

Does my sassiness upset you? D
Why are you beset with gloom? E
'Cause I walk like I've got oil wells F
Pumping in my living room. E

like moons — an example of a simile
like suns

Just like moons and like suns,
With the certainty of tides,
Just like hopes springing high,
Still I'll rise.

I'll rise (in the future)

Did you want to see me broken?
Bowed head and lowered eyes?
Shoulders falling down like teardrops,
Weakened by my soulful cries.

no hope in this verse

awful hard?

Colloquial abbreviation

Does my haughtiness offend you?
Don't you take it awful hard
'Cause I laugh like I've got gold mines
Diggin' in my own back yard.

three similes to do with earth's rich[es]

all the hurtful things you could do

like air

You may shoot me with your words,
You may cut me with your eyes,
You may kill me with your hatefulness,
But still, like air, I'll rise.

I'll rise (in the future)

Does my sexiness upset you?
Does it come as a surprise
That I dance like I've got diamonds
At the meeting of my thighs?

NB 4 line ver[se]

regular rhy[me] scheme up end of this verse

Short Sentence (I rise) contrasted with longer phrases (now in present)

Out of the huts of history's shame
I rise
Up from a past that's rooted in pain
I rise
I'm a black ocean, leaping and wide,
Welling and swelling I bear in the tide.

Why black?

hints of pregnancy and childbirth?

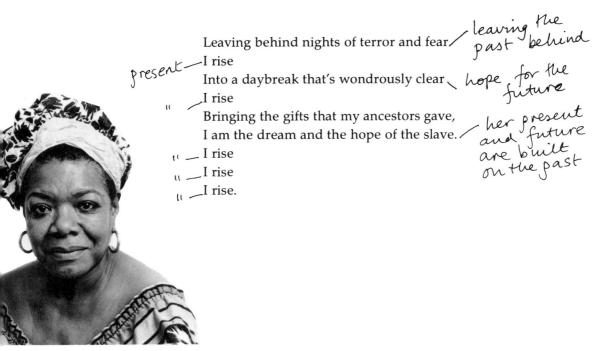

Leaving behind nights of terror and fear / *leaving the past behind*
present— I rise
Into a daybreak that's wondrously clear \ *hope for the future*
" ⎯ I rise
Bringing the gifts that my ancestors gave,
I am the dream and the hope of the slave. / *her present and future are built on the past*
" ⎯ I rise
" ⎯ I rise
" ⎯ I rise.

Throughout the poem Maya Angelou addresses you. She accuses you of bitter, twisted lies and says that you have trodden her in the dust and that you may shoot her, cut her, kill her.

> In your group discuss why she says this. Is she talking to each reader personally, or only some?

The imagery is mostly to do with the earth. It appears in similes (when one thing is compared to another) which begin with the word 'like'. (Similes can also begin with the word 'as'.) The effect of this imagery is to make the poem feel very basic, natural and earthy.

> In your group, identify three more similes and discuss their effect.

The tone is triumphant, challenging and optimistic. This is achieved by the declamatory style (it is like someone shouting at you), the way the structure changes in the last two verses and the vocabulary used.

> In your group discuss the way particular words and phrases build up to this effect.

■ PRIDE AND PREJUDICE

This is the opening of Jane Austen's novel.

It is a truth universally acknowledged, that a single man in possession of a fortune must be in want of a wife.

However little known the feelings or views of such a man may be on his first entering a neighbourhood, this truth is so well fixed in the minds of the surrounding families, that he is considered as the rightful property of some one or other of their daughters.

'My dear Mr Bennet,' said his lady to him one day, 'have you heard that Netherfield Park is let at last?'

Mr Bennet replied that he had not.

'But it is,' returned she; 'for Mrs Long has just been here, and she told me all about it.'

Mr Bennet made no answer.

'Do not you want to know who has taken it?' cried his wife impatiently.

'*You* want to tell me, and I have no objection to hearing it.'

This was invitation enough.

'Why, my dear, you must know, Mrs Long says that Netherfield is taken by a young man of large fortune from the north of England; that he came down on Monday in a chaise and four to see the place, and was so much delighted with it that he agreed with Mr Morris immediately; that he is to take possession before Michaelmas, and some of his servants are to be in the house by the end of next week.'

'What is his name?'

'Bingley.'

'Is he married or single?'

'Oh! single, my dear, to be sure! A single man of large fortune; four or five thousand a year. What a fine thing for our girls!'

'How so? how can it affect them?'

'My dear Mr Bennet,' replied his wife, 'how can you be so tiresome! You must know that I am thinking of his marrying one of them.'

In your group, list all the information that this passage gives you about the characters, the setting of the story, the situation and the plot.

Look at the first sentence; as an opening to a novel, this serves several purposes. There is a parody of a formal declaration, such as the opening passage of the American Constitution. There is also the contrast between the first and second halves of the sentence. The grand-sounding opening six words contrast sharply with the rather ordinary observation about marriage, which is not anyway 'universally acknowledged'. The sentence is ironic in tone; the author is not being entirely serious.

What other clues are there in the passage to suggest that the author is not being entirely serious?

There are words and phrases in the passage that you would not expect to find nowadays, such as: *in want of a wife*, *returned she*, *chaise*.

In your group, find some more examples of similarly archaic language.

It would be easy to imagine the situation described here as similar to an episode from *Coronation Street*, *EastEnders* or *Brookside*.

In your group, discuss what makes this passage different from a script of such programmes.

Bedtime Stories

At night we were wanderers
through a world of words

Travelling for the love of it
we would never hesitate
to stop and look around us
change direction
start afresh

Together we walked the main roads
and the less trod paths:
With him I learned
to use the signposts
read the maps

We were company

But I became impatient
discovered the thrill of speed
rejected his slow
unfolding of words
with all the extra meaning it could bring

I wanted to set my own pace
plan my own route

Slowly we drifted apart
went our separate ways
we travelled together
less often
and then not at all

I became a solitary explorer

journeyed far and journeyed fast
missed much
saw much

made my own way

He reads to my sister now
and sometimes
a world-weary nomad
I sneak into her room
and lie curled up on the floor

in companionable silence

Jenny Moy
Waverley School, London

Glesga

Noo tha' i's colt in o' Glesga toon,
Wains star' tae greet an' ge' bored pre'y soon,
Trains an' buses 'come mare an' mare terdy,
An' 'Dinkies' scoot passed with their swankey cers,
Ready fur wurk a' tall office blocks,
Wheel the Festival ge's pu' doon, a're a' the docks,
Un'er the Umbrella drunks lie in the stree's,
Then tae Cen'ral where 'wan' mee's.

A're a' 'Princes Squer', the 'trendies' gather,
Up tae the tope tae hev a wee blether,
Doon tae Merks tae buy year sokes,
Ye even pie fur the flippin pokes,
Roun' the pubs, ar' busy wi' cha'er
An' wipets si' ootside in the gu'er
Aye, i's colt doon 'ere in Glesga,
But i's ma hame, forever.

Gillian Wright
Westbourne School for Girls, Glasgow

This is where
we would have printed
your writing

Television Links

This section of the book aims to encourage active and critical viewing habits rather than passive reception. Stills from the programmes have been included to indicate appropriate places to pause and reflect on some of the complex issues raised.

Whose English?

English is spoken in different ways, with different accents and in different dialects. What accent do you have? What dialect? What attitudes do people have to their own, and other, accents and dialects?

Samantha Meah – Birmingham accent.
Robbie Coltrane – Glasgow accent.
Joanna Jones – Liverpool accent.
What is your accent? How would you describe it?

'When you say biscuit, you mean cookie, right?'
What differences do you notice between American English and British English?

Bob Hoskins describes four possible reactions to a Cockney accent. What is your reaction?

Listen to the comments of young people from London, Norfolk, Dorset, County Antrim, Yorkshire and Newcastle. Note any views you strongly agree or disagree with.

Bob Tite speaks with a Dorset accent and in a local dialect. For example: 'And he went to shake hands with me and it t'aint I 'tis he.'

Note some other examples of dialect from the programme.

'If I talked in a different accent I might not be able to express myself like I wanted to. Some words just fit in with you, don't they?' Is this true for you? Does the way you speak reflect your personality and identity?

The Hardest Thing You'll Ever Do

Learning to talk fluently and confidently takes most children about six years. Not all children make it, but for those that do, it is an amazing achievement.

This baby's first word is 'da'. Find examples of other words that toddlers are using in the programme. How important is the role of the parent or adult at this stage of learning?

Did you notice this boy's use of 'see-saw' to (a) ask a question, (b) make a statement and (c) express pleasure? How often do you use intonation to make your meaning clearer?

Some learning depends on imitation as we have seen with the reciting of nursery rhymes. Some learning definitely does not. Children do not hear adults say 'flied' or 'runned'. Why do children say these words?

Some children are learning two languages at once. What advantage does that have for these children?

Compare this girl telling a story with the girl at the start of the programme, or the boy who uses 'and' so often. In what ways has this girl developed as a speaker in comparison with them?

Can you explain what happens to a child who is autistic?

Ringing the Changes

A day in the life of Whitmore School. You will be able to consider the range of talk employed by a class of sixteen-year-olds and compare it with your own.

Do you ever role play?

In your pairs, act out one of the situations shown in the programme. Try using language you would not usually make use of and consider your use of facial gestures and body language.

Technical terms

Consider examples of technical terms that you have used this term in your particular school subjects.

Language for expressing emotion

As well as poetry and song, can you think of other examples of language being used to express emotion?

Collaborative talk

Discuss how often and in what situations you use collaborative talk.

Evaluating, explaining and justifying

Would you agree that the two students are doing all of these? Are they putting their language to other uses also?

Discuss how David's language changes from the informal talk in the playing field to the formal interview with the headteacher.

This programme has demonstrated the variety of achievement of students in speaking and listening. Reflect on your achievements in speaking and listening, reading and writing.

Talking Proper

The Queen's English, Received Pronunciation (RP), BBC English, Standard English. Are these descriptions for talking properly? Should you be talking differently?

The way the Queen speaks is called the Queen's English.
What sort of people speak with this accent?
Where do they live?

Here are some student reactions to the public school accent. Do you agree with any of them?

'If I talked like that I'd kill myself.'
'You're looking at money.'
'They were brought up to speak like that.'
'We stereotype them.'

Do you agree that what the four men were saying was 'degrading to women'?

BBC English.
What sort of people speak like this, other than BBC commentators?

'Advertisers can use our feelings about accents to sell their products.'
Which product do you think your accent could be used to sell?

Standard English is a dialect, not an accent.
Why has it achieved its current status?
Is it possible to speak Standard English with a regional accent?

Are there situations in which you would deliberately change your accent?
Discuss this question in relation to these comments from the programme:

'It's good to be able to change your accent.'
'People should be taken seriously, whatever their accent.'
'Adapt, but don't sell out.'
'Because I acquired a new accent, the backbone of my identity had been interfered with.'

Sticks and Stones

Why is language so controversial? This programme looks at some problem areas: swearing, sarcasm, verbal abuse and censorship.

Do you think swearing is ever justified?

Sarcasm. What is it and why is it hurtful?

Reflect on the discussion of racist and sexist language. How can this sort of language be stopped?

Is there too much bad language on television?
Is television a bad influence on young people's language?

Are there ever good reasons for censoring books?

■ *Trying to Connect You*

English has become a major world language. In many ways this has eased international communication. In other ways it is a source of tension and conflict.

Are you surprised at the extensive use of English as a world language, given that about one tenth of the world's population speak it as a first language?

What effect does TV have on people's language, here and around the world?

How might a further decline in the number of Welsh speakers be prevented?

Why was English such an important issue for the students of Soweto, in South Africa?

What Big Teeth You Have, Grammar

It isn't about being polite. It isn't about not making mistakes when you talk or write. It isn't about becoming a better speaker or writer. So what is grammar all about?

'Good manners?'
'Doing what you are told?'
What do you think 'grammar' is?

The rules of grammar are not like
the rules of a game.
How do we learn the rules of grammar?

'It is grammar that governs how words are strung together.'
What can humans, therefore, do with language that animals can't?

Make up a sentence that no one has probably ever used before.
Jumble up the words and give it to your partner to unravel.

Grammar is:

- the way words are put together to make sense.
- something we learn naturally as we grow up.
- an interesting aspect of language to investigate.

What three things do you need, according to the programme, to be a better writer and talker?

■ *In Your Hands*

Some processes and functions of writing examined: four reporters plan and write their first article for the school newspaper; a group of skateboarders campaign for a ramp in a local park; fifth-year students devise, write and perform their own scripted drama.

Four students planned, researched, discussed and finally wrote this article. What are the advantages of such collaboration? How often are you able to work in this way?

Posters, petitions and letters can all be forms of persuasion. What sorts of decisions did the skateboarders have to make in considering their purpose and audience, as they drafted each piece of writing?

The process started with a brain-storming session and ended with a performance. Explain and describe what happened in between, paying particular attention to the importance of talk.

Professional Boxers

This programme explores the differences between everyday language in use and language on television.

We eavesdrop on the mealtime conversation of a real-life family and compare the unscripted language of fly-on-the-wall documentary with the scripted language of soap, sitcom, news and advertisements.

How closely can television portray everyday language in use?

What are the differences between the language used by the fictional characters in *EastEnders* and that used by the real-life Wilkins family.

It's the little things that make it home OXO

'A family in Scunthorpe have foiled a bizarre bid by a mad axe-man . . .'
Discuss some of the examples of biased, sexist and emotive language in this 'news' broadcast.
N.B. Full text included below.

Discuss the differences between the language of this advertisement and the earlier ones that were shown.

A family in Scunthorpe have foiled a (bizarre) (murder) *illegal?*
(bid) by a (mad) axe-man. *sexist* *emotive*
colloquial *bias*
The horror attack took place as (pretty) brunette
Mary Jones, 36, was cooking a meal in the kitchen.

The axe-murderer:-

SMASHED into the house,
GRABBED terror-stricken Mrs Jones and
THREATENED her with the axe.

She was rescued by her hunky husband David, 40,
who threw the attacker to the ground. The axe-man then
escaped.

Stormed David: "He would have topped her, given half-a-
chance".

Stunned neighbours of the family dubbed the incident
"amazing", while police launched an immediate probe
into the attack.
loony left
~~Local~~ MP Reg Smith slammed the council's recent
decision to cut back on community policing, which
must have been responsible for a rise in local crime.
He exclusively revealed that crime figures had soared
recently.

Families in the area have been warned to look out
for a dangerous looking man in a green sweater.

If there are any developments in this exciting story,
we'll bring you more revelations later in the
programme.

The Heart of the Language

The television programme
includes dramatisations of the extracts in
Part 4 of the book. It is important that the
programme is viewed for pleasure and we
simply recommend that you pause at
the end of each performance. Watching
the programme should assist you with the
suggested activities in the book.

Glossary

ACCENT   We all speak with an accent, which is the way in which we pronounce words. Think of all the different ways that you have heard people pronounce words like *bath* or *down*. Accents usually tell us from which country and from which part of a country a speaker comes and often their social class.

COLLOQUIAL LANGUAGE   This is informal language of the sort we use in conversation rather than in formal writing.

CONNOTATIONS   These are meanings suggested by a word beyond its literal meaning, e.g. *weasel* suggests *cunning* or *sneakiness*.

CREOLE   When a pidgin language becomes the native language of a group of people and expands to include all the usual features of a language, it is called a creole. See PIDGIN.)

DIALECT   We all speak in a dialect. It refers to the words that we use and to particular variations in what we actually say. For example, in England they say *babies*; in Scotland they say *bairns*. While some people would say, 'He has done well', in London a Cockney would probably say, 'He done well'. Dialects usually tell us where someone is from and their social class.

DRAFTING   Each stage of a piece of writing from your earliest notes to your final version is called a *draft*. At each stage you will probably change parts after thinking about them carefully and perhaps discussing them with other people.

EUPHEMISM   This is a word or expression that you substitute for one that people might find offensive or upsetting, e.g. *departed* for *dead*.

GRAMMAR	People use this word to mean all sorts of different things but we are using it to refer to the rules that make it possible for you to convey meaning in a language, e.g. you need to know the order that words take in English if you want to be understood.
IDIOM	The English language is full of expressions that are used every day and do not literally mean what they say. These expressions are called idioms. Two examples are 'to give someone a piece of your mind' and 'to take someone for a ride'.
METALANGUAGE	This word describes the various terms that you need in order to be able to discuss language itself.
MORPHOLOGY	This is the term for the way in which a word can appear in different forms, e.g. *happy, happiness, unhappy.*
MOTHER TONGUE	If English is your mother tongue it means that it is the language that you learned to speak first. Some people call this your heritage language or home language.
PARODY	This is when you mimic the style of a type of speech or writing, often for humorous effect, e.g. writing a policeman's evidence as a rap. *I was proceeding down the Balls Pond Road* *When I saw a lorry with an unsecured load.*
PATOIS	This is a regional dialect of a language. It is often used to describe the various dialects to be found in the Caribbean islands.
PHONETIC SPELLING	If you want to write English to show the way in which the words are pronounced, you will need more than the 26 letters of the alphabet. The phonetic spelling of each word is in brackets. bet (bɛt) bat (bæt) bite (baɪt) but (bʌt) bout (baʊt)

PIDGIN	This is a simplified language used by people who do not understand each other's languages but need to communicate in order to trade. It is usually based on one of the languages and has no native speakers.
PREFIX	This is a letter or group of letters that can be attached to the beginning of a word to form a new word, e.g. un + happy = unhappy.
RECEIVED PRONUNCIATION (RP)	This is the accent of a particular social class and has no regional base. It is generally considered to be an upper-class accent.
SENTENCE	We could not find a satisfactory definition of this word; could you? (See page 74.)
SLANG	This is informal language, usually spoken rather than written, and is often used by a particular group of people with common interests or jobs.
STANDARD ENGLISH	This is a dialect once associated with the East Midlands region, which has become the language of government and trade and is usually accepted as the written form of the language in general use. You can speak Standard English with a Scots, Welsh, Jamaican or any other accent. It has acquired its status because it tends to be the dialect used by the most powerful people in society. Some people believe that it is the 'correct' way to speak English.
SUFFIX	A letter or group of letters added to the end of a word to form a new word, e.g. soft + ness = softness.
SYNTAX	This is the way in which words are organised in a sentence in order to make sense. Your own knowledge of syntactic rules enables you to know which sentences are, or are not, grammatical and to produce and understand an infinite number of sentences.
TRANSCRIPT	This is when you write down spoken language exactly as it was said.

PROGRAMMES OF STUDY FOR KNOWLEDGE ABOUT LANGUAGE

The chart below shows where the pages in the *Language File* book and television programmes match the programmes of study. We have not attempted to cover all of the programmes of study in detail and some units clearly relate more closely to a particular area than others. Unit 2, 'The Hardest Thing You'll Ever Do', and Unit 6, 'Trying to Connect You', deal with topics that we feel are neglected: Language Acquisition and Bilingualism.

Programmes of Study for speaking and listening	Language File Pages
Teaching about language through speaking and listening, which should have started by the time pupils are working towards **level 5**, should focus on:	**6-18** **18-28** **28-39** **40-54**
● regional and social variations in accents and dialects of the English language and attitudes to such variations;	**71-82** **93-102**
● the range of purposes which spoken language serves;	
● the forms and functions of spoken Standard English.	
In order to achieve **level 5**, pupils should be helped to make more extended contributions to group or class discussions and to informal or formal presentations, *eg. dramatic improvisation, role-play or scripted scenes*. They should be helped to make their questions more probing, and contributions to discussion more reasoned.	**6-18** **40-54**
Activities designed to develop pupils' knowledge about language should encourage discussion of vocabulary that is specific to:	
● local communities, *eg. words for local places, buildings, institutions, etc*;	
● local usages such as *bairn (cf. child), baps (cf. rolls), outwith (cf. outside)*;	
● particular age groups, *eg. frock (cf. dress), wireless (cf. radio)*;	
● certain occupations, *eg. the specialist terms and acronyms used by groups such as doctors, mechanics, builders, computer experts and lawyers*.	
In order to achieve **level 6**, pupils should be encouraged to work in a wider range of situations in which their individual contributions are given greater emphasis. Pupils should be guided towards the use of spoken Standard English in public or formal situations.	**6-18** **40-54**
Pupils should be given the opportunity to consider:	
● people's sensitivity to features of pronunciation that differentiate the speech of one area from others;	

	Language File Pages
● any grammatical differences between the speech of the area and spoken Standard English, *eg. in verb forms, pronouns use, prepositions*.	
In order to achieve **level 7**, pupils should participate extensively in widely varied group work in a range of groupings.	**28-39** **40-54** **82-93**
Pupils should consider:	**93-102** **102-113**
● language appropriate to situation, topic and purpose;	
● how inappropriate language can be a source of humour (either intentional or unintentional), or may give a false impression of the speaker or writer.	
Pupils should be taught:	
● that Standard English is the language of wide social communication;	
● that Standard English is generally required in public or formal settings;	
● through discussion, about the situations and purposes for which people might use non-standard varieties rather than Standard English: *eg. in speech with friends, in a local team or group, in television advertising, folk songs, poetry, dialogue in novels or plays*.	
In order to achieve **level 9**, pupils should be helped to recognise that speech ranges from intimate or casual spontaneous conversation, *eg. jokes, anecdotes, banter, gossip, argument*, through discussion, commentary and debate to more formal forms, such as *lectures and sermons, toasts and oaths*.	**6-18** **28-39** **93-102**
In order to achieve **level 10**, pupils should be helped to recognise that attitudes to Standard English and to non-standard varieties, *eg. as expressed in letters to newspapers*, can be based on stereotypes and prescriptive judgement. Teaching at this level should make more explicit what has been previously noted incidentally, ie. how language can be a bond between members of a group, a symbol of national pride, a barrier and a source of misunderstandings, and can be used to alienate, insult, wound, offend, praise or flatter, be polite or rude. At this level these matters might be the subject of more systematic analytical and historical study.	**6-18** **40-54** **54-60** **60-71** **93-102**

PROGRAMMES OF STUDY FOR READING

In order to achieve **level 5** . . .   **93–102**
Teachers should discuss texts which make   **102–113**
imaginative use of English – literature,
advertising, songs, etc – in order to bring out the
ways in which the choice of words affects the
impression given by the text. Pupils should
consider: the way word meanings can be played
with, *eg. in riddles, puns, jokes, spoonerisms, word
games, graffiti, advertisements, poems*; the use of
nonsense words and deliberate misspellings, *eg.
in poems and advertisements.*

Teaching of knowledge about language through   **6–18**
reading should focus on: **40–54**
- some of the main characteristics of literary   **71–82**
  language and how it conveys meanings;   **102–113**
- some of the ways in which English is
  constantly changing between generations and
  over the centuries; and people's attitudes to
  such change.

In order to achieve **level 6**, pupils should be   **6–18**
reading some texts not written specifically for   **40–54**
children or young people.   **60–70**
Pupils should discuss: **71–82**

- examples of words and expressions which
  tend to undergo very rapid change in use or
  meaning, *eg. terms of approbation ('wicked',
  'brill'.)*;
- differences in the use and meanings of words
  used by pupils, their parents and
  grandparents, *eg. wireless, radio, tranny, receiver*;
- new words that have become part of the
  English vocabulary during the last 50 years or
  so, *eg. computer, astronaut, macho*;
- the reasons why vocabulary changes over
  time, *eg. contact with other languages because of
  trade or political circumstances, fashion, effects of
  advertising, need for new euphemisms, new
  inventions and technology, changes in society*;
- where new words come from, *eg. coinages,
  acronyms, or borrowings from other languages
  ('glasnost', 'catamaran', 'chic').*

In order to achieve **level 7**, pupils should read   **102–113**
some texts written for adults, including pre-20th
century fiction, poetry and drama, including
Shakespeare. Discussion of those texts should
include the literary style, as well as themes,
settings and characters.

In both fiction and non-fiction texts, they should
be taught to use information or contextual clues
to deduce authorial points of view. Non-literary
texts used should include persuasive writing, *eg.
advertisements, leader columns from newspapers,
campaign literature from pressure groups*, and
reference books, *eg. where the subject matter has a
logical structure rather than following a chronological
order.*

Pupils should discuss a variety of works so as to
bring out the range and effects of different types
of sound patterning, *eg. alliteration, assonance,
rhymes, onomatopoeia*, and of figures of speech, *eg.
similes, metaphors, personification.*

In order to achieve **level 8** . . .   **40–54**
From their reading of pre-20th century literature,   **71–82**
pupils should be encouraged to identify some of   **102–113**
the major changes in English grammar over the
centuries, *eg. the loss – except in some dialects and in
religious uses – of 'thee' and 'thou'*; the
simplification of the verb system, *eg. from 'have',
'hast', 'hath', to 'have' and 'has'*; the change in
structure of negatives, *eg. from 'I know not' to 'I
don't know'.*

In order to achieve **level 9**, pupils should be   **71–82**
taught how to analyse documents critically.   **102–113**
Teachers should discuss the cogency and clarity
of such documents and should encourage pupils
to improve them. Pupils should be made aware
of the subtler uses of language, and of the
appropriate use of figures of speech.

Pupils should discuss:

- the effects, in context, of different types of
  vocabulary, *eg. archaic, literary, figurative,
  emotive, dialectal, colloquial, scientific, etc*;
- grammatical features such as structural
  repetition, *eg. in scripted speeches,
  advertisements, literary prose, poems, etc*;
- ambiguity, either of vocabulary or
  grammatical structure;
- the use of grammatical deviance for special
  effect, *eg. in advertisements, slogans, poems, etc.*

In order to achieve **level 10**, pupils should   **6–18**
discuss the possibility of multiple meanings in   **40–54**
the texts studied and be taught how to recognise   **71–82**
and describe some of them.

Pupils should consider not only the extent to
which English has changed from the earliest
written records, but also ways in which it is
changing now. From this, they will be helped to
recognise that judgements about what is
appropriate or correct do not remain constant.
They should be shown how to recognise when
people's attitudes to language use, *eg. as expressed
in letters to newspapers*, reveal misunderstandings
about the nature of language change.

PROGRAMMES OF STUDY FOR WRITING

In order to acheive **level 5**, pupils should be helped to extend their range of vocabulary and to increase their awareness of what is suitable according to purpose and context, *eg. the kinds of topics and situations in which slang is used; the need for specialist terms and the effects of their use outside the specialist group.* Discussion should bring out contrasts in how vocabulary is used in speech and writing.

28–39
40–54
82–93

In order to achieve **level 6**, pupils should come to understand the functions of the impersonal style of writing such as might be used in academic – and particularly scientific – writing and to recognise the linguistic features, *eg. the passive, subordination*, which characterise it. This should be done by reading and discussing examples.

28–39
71–82
82–93

Teaching should bring out the fact that as speech typically takes place in a situation where both speaker and listener are present, it can be accompanied by gestures and words like 'this', 'that', 'here', 'now', 'you', etc, whereas writing generally requires greater verbal explicitness. Pupils should be helped to recognise that because writers are not able to use the voice to emphasise key points in a sentence, they have to use a wide range of grammatical structures (such as the passive, or other alterations of word order) to bring about the desired emphasis. They should also recognise that writing is often more formal and more impersonal than speech: lexical and grammatical features of language both reflect and create these contrasts.

In order to achieve **level 7**, pupils should develop a sensitivity to the different styles of vocabulary that are used in different types of writing.

18–28
28–39
82–93
101–113

Pupils should be taught about the different functions of written language: that writing can be for the writer alone; it can be addressed to a known reader; or it can be written for a large and unknown audience. They should be shown how it may primarily be either an artefact in its own right or a means of conveying information; how it functions as a tool of thought and as a creator of human relationships; how it can be stored and readily transmitted across time and distance. They should be helped to think of appropriateness in written language in terms of these functions and of the range of audiences that writers address, considering the effects, for example, of inappropriately formal vocabulary in personal letters or of colloquial expressions in impersonal writing.

In order to achieve **level 8** pupils should come to understand that, at its most characteristic, speech is interactive, spontaneous and informal which means that topics of conversation emerge in an unplanned and unstructured way; in contrast, writing needs a more tightly planned structure signalled by the organisation of topics into paragraphs and words and phrases such as *'meanwhile', 'in the same way'*, and *'on the other hand'*.

82–93

They should be helped to recognise the patterns of organisation of formal expository writing: *eg. the introduction, development and conclusion of the academic essay; the use of illsutrations and examples in persuasive writing and of comparison and contrast in argument.*

In order to achieve **level 9**, pupils should be taught:

28–39
71–82
82–93
93–102

● how to recognise and describe some of the lexical, grammatical and organisational characteristics of different types of written texts, *eg. letters, tabloid and broadsheet newspapers, teenage magazines, specialist hobby periodicals, holiday brochures, travel books, instructions, playscripts;*

● about the nature and purpose of impersonal styles of writing, and the vocabulary and grammar characteristic of those styles, *eg. the use of the passive voice and of other ways of depersonalising text – such as not using pronouns.*

In order to achieve **level 10**, pupils should be taught, in the context of their own writing and that of a range of published writers, that, in evaluating the success of a piece of writing, different criteria need to be applied to different types; for example, a personal letter may be valued for its warmth and humour, a report for the clarity of its organisation, etc.

71–82
82–93

ATTAINMENT TARGETS FOR KNOWLEDGE ABOUT LANGUAGE

These attainment targets are concerned only with knowledge about language. We have covered many other attainment targets in our units but we have not included them in the chart below.

KEY
SL = Speaking and Listening
R = Reading
W = Writing
Numbers refer to levels

UNIT	
1 Whose English? (pages 6–18)	Recognise variations in vocabulary between different regional or social groups. (SL5)
	Show in discussion of their reading awareness that words can change in use and meaning over time and demonstrate some of the reasons why. (R6)
	Demonstrate in discussion and in writing some understanding of attitudes in society towards language change and of ideas about appropriateness and correctness in language use. (R10)
2 The Hardest Thing You'll Ever Do (pages 18–28)	Show in discussion an awareness of the appropriate use of spoken language, according to purpose, topic and audience. (SL7)
	Show in discussion and in writing an awareness of the contribution that facial expressions, gestures and tone of voice can make to a speaker's meaning. (SL8)
	Show in discussion and in writing an awareness of some of the factors that influence people's attitudes to the way other people speak. (SL10)
3 Ringing the Changes (pages 28–39)	Show in discussion an awareness of the appropriate use of spoken language, according to purpose, topic and audience. (SL7)
	Show in discussion and in writing an awareness of the ways in which language varies between different types of spoken communication. (SL9)
	Demonstrate in discussion and writing some understanding of attitudes in society towards language change and of ideas about appropriateness and correctness in language use. (R10)

4 Talking Proper
(pages 40–54)

Recognise variations in vocabulary between different regional or social groups. (SL5)

Show in discussion an awareness of grammatical differences between spoken Standard English and a non-standard variety. (SL6)

Show in discussion and in writing an awareness of some of the factors that influence people's attitudes to the way other people speak. (SL10)

Show in discussion of their reading an awareness that words can change in use and meaning over time and demonstrate some of the reasons why. (R6)

Demonstrate in discussion and in writing some understanding of attitudes in society towards language change and of ideas about appropriateness and correctness in language use. (R10)

5 Sticks and Stones
(pages 54–60)

Show in discussion and in writing an awareness of the contribution that facial expressions, gestures and tone of voice can make to a speaker's meaning. (SL8)

Show in discussion and in writing an awareness of some of the factors that influence people's attitudes to the way other people speak. (SL10)

Show in discussion of their reading an awareness that words can change in use and meaning over time and demonstrate some of the reasons why. (R6)

6 Trying to Connect You
(pages 60–70)

Show in discussion and in writing an awareness of some of the factors that influence people's attitudes to the way other people speak. (SL10)

7 What Big Teeth
You Have, Grammar
(pages 71–82)

Discuss and write about changes in the grammar of English over time, encountered in the course of their reading. (R8)

Demonstrate, through discussion and in their writing, grammatical differences between spoken and written English. (W6)

Demonstrate, in discussion and in writing, knowledge of criteria by which different types of written language can be judged. (W10)

8 In Your Hands
(pages 82–93)

Demonstrate some understanding of the use of lexical and grammatical effects in language of literature. (R9)

Show in discussion the ability to recognise variations in vocabulary according to purpose, topic and audience and whether language is spoken or written and use them appropriately in their writing. (W5)

Demonstrate, through discussion and in their writing, grammatical differences between spoken and written English. (W6)

Show in discussion and in writing an awareness of what is appropriate and inappropriate language in written texts. (W7)

Demonstrate knowledge of organisational differences between spoken and written English. (W8)

Demonstrate in discussion and in writing knowledge of ways in which language varies between different types of written text. (W9)

Demonstrate in discussion and in writing knowledge of criteria by which different types of written language can be judged. (W10)

9 Professional Boxers
(pages 93–102)

Show in discussion and in writing an awareness of the contribution that facial expressions, gestures and tone of voice can make to a speaker's meaning. (SL8)

10 The Heart of the Language
(pages 102–113)

Show through discussion an awareness of a writer's choice of particular words and phrases and the effect on the reader. (R5)

Show in discussion or in writing an awareness of writters' use of sound patterns and some other literary devices and the effect on the reader. (R7)

Acknowledgement is due to the following whose permission is required for multiple reproduction:

THE SOCIETY OF AUTHORS on behalf of the Bernard Shaw Estate for *Pygmalion*; METHUEN DRAMA for an extract from *Educating Rita* by Willy Russell; *Listen Mr Oxford Don* reprinted by permission of John Agard c/o Caroline Sheldon Literacy Agency, from Mangoes and Bullets (Serpents Tail) 1985 © John Agard 1985; WILLIAM MORRIS AGENCY (UK) LTD for television comedy scripts by Dick Clements and Ian le Frenais; PETERS, FRASER & DUNLOP for 'Her Big Chance' from *Talking Heads* by Alan Bennett; 'Making Cocoa for Kingsley Amis' by Wendy Cope reprinted by permission of Faber and Faber Ltd; WARNER CHAPPELL MUSIC LTD for *Throw The 'R' Away* by The Proclaimers; MICHAEL ROSEN for his poem on p. 78; 'And Still I Rise' © Maya Angelou published by VIRAGO PRESS LTD 1986; CADBURY LTD for 'Glesga', taken from *Cadbury's 7th Book of Children's Poetry*; CROOM HELM LTD for illustration on p. 19; OCTOPUS CHILDREN'S PUBLISHING for the extract from *The Jolly Postman* by Janet and Allan Ahlberg; PYTHON (MONTY) PICTURES for an extract from 'The Parrot Sketch'.

Photographic credits
Page **8** Kobal Collection; **9** Random House UK Ltd; **10** (left) Press Association; (centre left) Colorsport; (centre right) Hutton Management Ltd, Roger Morton; **40** Crysalis Records; **43** Mansell Collection; **51** Courtesy South Bank Centre; **59** Python Monty Pictures, John Sims; **61** (top) Mary Evans Picture Library; **61** (bottom), **62** and **63** Hulton-Deutsch Collection; **64A** Barnaby's Picture Library; **64B, D, F** and **H** Network Photographers; **64C** and **E** Sally & Richard Greenhill; **64G** Photo Co-op; **68** Courtesy I.L.E.A.; **91** Barnaby's Picture Library; **93** (left) Channel 4 Television; **93** (bottom) Granada Television; **96** (centre top) London Weekend Television; **109** Virago Press Ltd.

All other pictures including the Television Links section and cover © BBC.